WHEN A HUG WON'T FIX THE HURT

Walking with Your Child Through Crisis

KAREN DOCKREY

New Hope® Publishers
P.O. Box 12065
Birmingham, AL 35202-2065
www.newhopepubl.com

Dockrey, Karen, 1955–
When a hug won't fix the hurt/by Karen Dockrey.
p.   cm.
ISBN 1-56476-062-6
1.   Sick children—Mental health. 2. Parenting. 3. Parenting—Religious aspects—Christianity. 4. Adjustment (Psychology).
I.Title
RJ47.5.D63 1993
649.8—dc20

Cover design by Theresa Barnett
Cover photo by Karim Shamsi-Basha

ISBN: 1-56309-495-9
N014106•0102•2M2

Dedicated to

Emily, Sarah, Allison, Katherine, and Drew,
who have taught us the persistence of joy
in the midst of pain

and to

the caring professionals who work
in partnership with us to rear our children
healthy, happy, and equipped to meet the
challenges they face. These people include
Rebecca Fisher; John Lukens; Kenneth
Wyatt; Gary Jackson; Ann Sitton;
Jerry Crook, Sr.; Ann; Connie;
Becky; and Terry.

Contents

Introduction

Every Crisis Counts

"Jesus wept. Then the Jews said,
'See how He loved him!' "
John 11:35–36

B oth of my children deal with intense crises, my ten-year-old with leukemia and my seven-year-old with severe hearing loss. Even with these ever-present crises, I have discovered that, at least for the moment, the everyday crises such as dealing with a difficult teacher or enduring a painful ear infection impact my children just as deeply as the lifelong crises. Any crisis, whether major or minor, continuing or short-term, requires skillful parenting. Crises can bring unity or division, growth or decline as a family, progression or regression, closeness to God or alienation from Him. This book is designed to help you maximize the positives and minimize the negatives. Through sharing experiences of real parents and children, this book attempts to help you love, equip, and walk with your children through the crises that confront them.

It's OK to struggle—both as a parent and with your child. As you invite God along, He'll love you and equip your whole family to face what comes. God can understand because He has suffered. God can equip because He is all-powerful. God can give hope because He is Hope. God can give joy because no evil is strong enough to quench Him.

As 2 Corinthians 4:8-9 explains, "We are hard pressed on every side, but not crushed; perplexed, but not in despair; persecuted, but not abandoned; struck down, but not destroyed." *When a Hug Won't Fix the Hurt* explores ways parents and children can live this promise no matter what the crisis. It illustrates faith in God without giving pat answers or explaining away the anguish. It suggests actions that enable families to maintain their routines while allowing time to grieve and to heal. It weaves Bible truth with experience to show how to walk through pain toward healing and wholeness. It shares answers others have found to enable them to move ahead and live fully.

A crisis can last a single day, such as a falling out with a friend; or a lifetime, such as the continuing challenges faced by a child with a disability. Crisis means intensity. A crisis can be chaos coupled with joy, such as the birth of a child or the blending of two families. A crisis can be brief but terrifying, such as an accident requiring an emergency room visit. A crisis can bring positive changes, such as beginning elementary, middle, or high school. A crisis can bring painful changes, such as divorce or long-term illness. A crisis can be life-enriching, such as the anxiety that comes with learning a new skill and the consequent competence that comes with mastering it. A crisis can be life-wrenching, such as the death of a parent or friend. *When a Hug Won't Fix the Hurt* illustrates ways children walk through crises like these and tells how families can work together to meet the challenges of the crisis.

You don't have to be superhuman or even super-spiritual to parent a child through crisis. You simply have to value your child and provide the tools she needs. Your compassionate presence, loving care, and steady guidance are critical to your child making it through unscarred. All children need certain expressions of this love—these are summarized by the titles of the ten chapters. But the specific ways you meet these needs are up to God and you. As you learn from the families in this book, discover a style that matches your child.

In many ways parenting is synonymous with crisis. We guide our children to respond in redemptive ways to both the happy and sad events of their lives. We help traumas be less traumatic, soothe tragedies with hope, provide skills to surmount the obstacles, and walk together through pain. We parents can respond with steadiness and creativity, or we can panic and make things worse. Let's be intentional about our responsibility to guide, equip, listen to, answer, and encourage our precious one-of-a-kind children.

Though the stories in this book are real, most names have been changed to protect the privacy of the persons involved.

Chapter 1

Respond to Feelings

"If it's mentionable, it's manageable."
–Fred Rogers

After waking early, laying out her practice clothes, and repeatedly asking, "Is it time yet?" seven-year-old Sarah returned from her first soccer practice discouraged and despondent.

"I'm never going to soccer practice again! I hate it and it's no fun."

"You were really frustrated, huh?" I responded.

"Yes! It wasn't any fun and it was too long. I hate it," said Sarah.

"Remember Emily's first couple of basketball practices? She was confused and frustrated. The first time is always a little hard," I suggested.

"No, I don't remember her first basketball practice. But I hate soccer. I'm never going back," repeated Sarah.

Emily, Sarah's sister, rapidly added, "But if you don't play, you won't get to be in the mother/daughter soccer game."

"I don't care. I'm not going back," persisted Sarah.

At that moment Sarah really didn't care. Logic and facts mattered little. All she could see was her own anguish and confusion over learning something new.

That night I had trouble sleeping. I imagined Sarah slamming the ball successfully into the goal. My happy dream melted as I recalled her confused face and heard her repeat, "What did he [the coach] say? I can't understand him." I saw her run to the goal and kick the ball outside the goal rather than in it. I heard her ask me what we'd have for supper rather than pay attention to the drill. I logically reminded myself that all first season soccer players have trouble hitting the goal, that all young children find an hour practice too long, that all children prefer asking questions to repeating drills. But the old, familiar pain had returned—the realization that Sarah's hearing loss meant struggling to hear and understand in every new situation. I experienced afresh the discovery that Sarah could not hear without hearing aids, that even under the best of circumstances she would miss 15-20 percent of what is said. I realized once again that the hearing crisis was not over.

My pain continued as I worried that the coach wouldn't want to help Sarah, that he'd rather have a better player, that the other players would resent her lack of skill. Then I remembered Sarah's friendliness—the ease with which she makes and keeps friends. I recalled the many times she had put people at such ease that they forgot she was hard-of-hearing. I also reminded myself that soccer skill has nothing to do with hearing. I anticipated that one or two more practices would increase her skill. I recalled the names of the other new or average players.

These facts helped some. But tonight Sarah had acted shy. Tonight she had spoken to no one but me. Tonight she was frustrated and angry. Tonight she was in pain, so I was in pain.

Sarah awoke the next morning preparing for another practice. She laid out her shin guards, checked the late February weather hoping it would be warm enough to wear shorts, and filled her water bottle. "I hope you and Daddy know I really do want to play soccer. I was just . . . you know, playing a little joke last night."

I forced myself to respond through my still-aching heart, "Yes, you were very frustrated. And that's OK. Everyone has trouble during the first practice. It will get better each time. If you have trouble hearing directions, ask questions or follow the lead of the other girls. I know you can do it."

This morning Sarah was ready to hear solutions. Last night she wasn't. I would have been denying her pain to explain it away with, "You'll feel better in the morning." Last night she needed me to understand her crisis and feel her pain. I found it all too easy to do the latter.

ACCEPT THE PAIN

We parents have trouble accepting our children's painful feelings because pain is hard. We don't want our children to hurt. We want them to breeze through a worry-free childhood. So we try to explain the pain away with easy-sounding solutions. We try to erase any worries with happy-sounding clichés. But even our best efforts can't change the fact that anger, sadness, frustration, and fear are real. Whether we like them or not, sad emotions are normal and important feelings. God gave us these feelings for good reasons. As Sarah and other children express their feelings, especially the scary ones, they gain the ability to handle them, and they discover what to do about them. When we parents deny our children this privilege, we force them to suffer alone.

Certainly we want a pain-free existence for our children. But pain is a part of life on this earth. Children hurt. Children want to talk about how they feel and what they think. Children need our support, interpretation, equipping, advocacy, and motivation. Refuse to let your uneasiness or fear deny your children these very important needs.

As we feel pain with our children and invite God along to comfort, advise, and equip us, we become able to attack the pain with reality. God reminds me that Sarah needs the sports experiences that other children have, that playing on a team will teach her valuable cooperation and confidence skills, that enjoying soccer will give her one more way to forget about her hearing loss and concentrate on living. He assures me that even when these new experiences are painful to me, I must, for Sarah's sake, go through the pain. Giving in to my fears and taking her off the team will keep her from experiencing life at its fullest.

Because we parents feel our children's pain, we often let our own anguish cloud theirs. We don't have to. As we parents identify how our children's crises impact us, we can make our way through the fog of our own struggles to see clearly enough to give the support, skills, companionship, and motivation they need. And, with God's help, both our needs are met.

IDENTIFY THE FEELING BEHIND THE WORDS

Rebecca, anguishing over her mother's car accident, blurted out, "I hate God for letting this happen!"

"You can't hate God, Rebecca!" her startled dad reacted.

"But I do. He caused Mom to be in a coma. Pat said God must have given the accident so Mom could rest. But I don't think Mom wanted to rest that way! We need her here," said Rebecca.

Collecting his thoughts, her dad continued, "I must disagree with Pat. It was the drunk driver, not God, who caused the accident. God didn't give this accident. I think He's as sad about it as we are."

"I'm still mad that He let it happen," said Rebecca.

"That's OK. God can handle the anger. In fact, when you tell God your feelings, He can help you heal. He's on your side, Rebecca, not working against you," assured Dad.

"I sure hope so," said Rebecca, relieved that at least someone was still there for her.

Rebecca was shaken and scared. Her mom wasn't around, and she wondered if God even cared. In the midst of her pain she yelled at God, angry that He hadn't kept her life safe and happy. She couldn't understand why He hadn't changed things. Her dad's initial reaction didn't help much, but he moved on to respond more appropriately. Quite honestly, he felt the same way. He also feared that, in her anger, Rebecca would cut God off. But he remembered that it's OK to get mad at God. God knows that anger is a sign of pain. As Rebecca shares her feelings with God, He can heal and comfort her. Rebecca's dad helped this healing process by listening, by explaining, and by understanding her anger. He gently guided her to direct her anger toward the right target—alcohol or the drunk driver, or even the devil, who delights in such things.

Like Rebecca, most children are unashamedly honest. Avoid saying to your children, "You don't really mean that," or "Don't feel that way!" Feelings are feelings. It's what we do with them that counts. As your child tells you about her anger, pain, and fear, identify what's behind her words and guide her to discover what to do about it.

Child's Viewpoint

Children don't evaluate the rightness or wrongness of feelings. They simply feel them. Whether they are experiencing ecstasy or agony, children feel fully. Refuse to take away this honest approach to life. Instead, guide your child to respond to his feelings in God-honoring ways.

Loneliness was behind Rebecca's angry outburst. She missed her mom and all the ways her mom cared for her. As Rebecca's dad identified this, he was better able to respond to Rebecca's anger. Rebecca didn't like her anger. It scared her. She needed her dad to help her through it and give her a sense of safety.

"I hate you, I hate you, I hate you!" said Louis to his mom.

"Why do you hate me?" responded Mom.

"Because you never let me do what I want to do."

"Like what?" asked Mom.

"Like eat the foods I like," said Louis.

"You're mad because you have to eat broccoli tonight?" guessed Mom.

"Yes. It's not fair!" declared Louis.

Obviously Louis does not hate his mom, nor is it true that she never lets him do what he wants to do. But arguing this point is not the way to help Louis. Instead, Louis's mom wisely helped Louis recognize the reason for his anger. He felt powerless, and that powerlessness translated to hate for the one with power. By responding the way she did, Louis's mom freed Louis from hate. He could then turn to her for help with his dilemma.

"Why don't you eat it first and wash it down with lots of milk," Mom suggested. "Then eat the foods you like. That will put the good taste in your mouth at the end. That's what I did when I was little."

"You hated broccoli, too?" asked Louis, amazed.

"Yes, and green beans," confessed Mom.

By noticing the feeling, sharing strategies, and identifying with the feeling, Louis's mom built camaraderie rather than antagonism. She demonstrated respect for Louis, a crucial action that many parents forget. Our children are people, not extensions of us or bothersome whiners. Respecting Louis made his scary feelings of hate go away. It gave him the power and strategy he needed to handle his problem.

Equally important, Louis's mom stayed true to her original demand. She didn't excuse Louis from eating his broccoli simply because he got mad. She gave him a method for eating. Feelings are not a way to manipulate people or change the circumstances. They're an invitation for help.

Beth hates the allergy shots she has to take. "I hate that nurse. Why does she do that to me?" accused Beth.

"You hate the needles and the pain they cause?" responded Dad.

"Yes. When I grow up, I'm going to invent a way to give shots without a needle," said Beth.

"Sounds good to me; I'll be the first to take one. I hate needles, too," said Dad. "For now, let's get through it and get out of here."

"Yeah!" said Beth.

Children attach fear and anger to the people who cause pain. As children talk about their feelings, parents can help children understand the source of their fear and discover how to cope with it.

Feelings loom large at night, when children are alone and when they are worried. Especially during times of crisis, check in with your children thirty minutes after they go to bed, when they get unusually quiet, and when a tough time is coming up. "What's on your mind?" or "How are you feeling about tomorrow?" invites your child to tell you what he needs. As you listen, interpret, and suggest, you can meet the needs behind the feelings. You can be the catalyst for helping scary feelings become manageable.

RECOGNIZE THE FEELINGS BEHIND THE ACTIONS

Your child might not use words to express her feelings. She might show her worry with silliness, her fear with anger, her anxiety with incessant talking. Or she may assign her fear to someone else:

"I think Sam and I better sleep together in case he gets scared," suggested Kathryn after learning that her grandpa had been hospitalized.

"What might Sam be afraid of?" asked Daddy.

"It probably wouldn't happen, but he might be scared of going to the hospital, too," offered Kathryn.

After confirming that illness is not the cause when your child is excessively silly, anxious, or angry, try questions and actions like these:

"What's happened at school lately?" "What's coming up?"

Work a puzzle or do a project together. Together projects give the opportunity to talk without the pressure to talk.

"What have you been thinking or wondering about lately?"

Talk to each other with puppets. Children will often say with a puppet what they'll never say directly.

> Feelings are not a way to manipulate people or change the circumstances. They're an invitation for help.

"What's the best and worst thing that has happened to you lately?"

Play with miniature figures using a play school, home, or work setting. Your child may share his feelings by talking for the figures.

Even with questions, your child may not be able to verbalize his feelings. That's OK. Most sad or scary feelings can be eased with some extra assurance and TLC.

Shortly after Ginger scooped her fussy toddler into her lap for some rocking and reading, he fell asleep. His crisis was fatigue.

When Ben and his grouchy daughter take a walk together, she calms down. Ben doesn't always find out what has been bothering her, but his attention seems to solve whatever it was.

Andrew invites his stepbrother Ray to play basketball when he gets angry. The activity of the game calms Ray enough to talk about what's bothering him.

Many children would rather write or draw their feelings than say them. Amanda's wise grandmother gave her a diary shortly after Amanda was diagnosed with cancer. Though Amanda usually talked freely, she took her diary with her to all treatments, writing furiously both before and after the shots. She then gave her diary to her parents to read.

After her friend Amy's death, Amanda wrote this poem to remember her by:

Amy we miss you
Amy I swear
Amy we care
Amy we're mad
Amy we're sad
Amy we'll get you
and take you away from there.

She also drew picture after picture of sadness, of Amy's name, and of memories. Whether your child talks about his crises or not, provide plentiful paper, markers, and pencils. Keep these materials handy at all times to ensure that your child will have them when he needs them.

HOLD AND CRY ALONG

Amanda responded with shock when her mother told her that her friend Amy had died. Amanda watched television for an hour, crying quietly in her daddy's lap. Later, a dam of tears exploded. Through tears she wailed,

"I don't ever want to go to McDonald's again."

Through tears, her mother responded, "Going to McDonald's would make you sad because it will remind you of Amy?"

"Yes. I never want to go again," Amanda said.

"We don't have to," her mother said. "You may feel like going later, but we don't have to go until you feel like it."

Her mother shares, "Everything in me wanted to fight against the reality of Amy's death. Everything in me wanted to stop Amanda's pain, to say it was all OK, to say she didn't have to be so sad. But Amy's death is real, and Amanda's pain is a sign of love for Amy. I do both girls a disservice when I try to push Amanda's grief away. I wanted to say, 'Of course you want to go to McDonald's. You love the food. We can have happy memories of Amy there.' But I checked myself long enough to recognize the pain behind Amanda's words."

A friend, surprised that Amanda's pain over Amy's death was so long-lasting, explained that even Christians are human enough to hurt. I prefer to believe there's nothing un-Christian about pain. Jesus, who knew Lazarus would be raised from death in minutes, cried tears of grief (John 11:35). Those watching understood Jesus' tears as a sign of Jesus' love for Lazarus (11:36). Assure your children that pain is an aspect of love: we can't hurt if we don't care.

As she cried along, Amanda's mother said, "Even though it hurts so much to lose Amy, I would rather have known her for a little while than not at all."

"Me, too. What will they do with her stuff? Maybe I can have Barney to remember her by," said Amanda.

Barney was a stuffed cat that Amanda had given Amy. Amy's mom gladly gave the cat to Amanda. Now Barney stands proudly on Amanda's dresser as a bittersweet reminder of a dear friend. Barney stands alongside a stuffed cat of Amanda's, a testimony that one day Amanda and Amy will be together in heaven. There they'll never have to say good-bye.

Grief is a painful feeling that has no quick or easy solution. Hope, companionship, and expressed feelings help; but we simply have to walk through it. Psalm 23:4 assures us that we can go through grief safely because of God's steady care. "Even though I walk through the valley of the shadow of death, I will fear no evil, for You are with me; Your rod and Your staff, they comfort me."

BE HONEST

In the process of helping children understand their painful feelings, be honest. Don't ever deceive with false promises or wishful thinking. This well-meaning widow tried to ease her son's fears of death:

"How could you have let Daddy die?" said Juan.

"He died before we could get to the doctor," explained Mom.

"Will you let me die?" wondered Juan.

"No. I always take you to the doctor right away, and the doctor helps you get well. We won't let you die," said Mom.

Though this mom and all moms wish these words could be true, no doctor can fix every problem. Children do die. Better would be, "It would be very unusual for you to die young. Your doctor and I take care of you to keep that from happening. But if you do die young, Jesus will take you to heaven and take care of you. I would be very sad, and I would miss you deeply just like we miss Daddy."

Your child might continue, "But I don't want to die!"

"And I don't want you to. You probably won't die young, because most people die when they're older. But we all will die sometime. I want you to know what happens after death so you don't have to be afraid of death. Jesus will take care of us both before and after we die."

"But I want you to take care of me."

"So do I. And most of the time, that's what happens."

Death is an uncomfortable reality. But we must admit that it is real. By addressing your child's fears honestly, you give him real answers that really work.

When your child asks hard questions about death and other forms of pain, answer as honestly as you can.

"Why did you have to tell me that Amy died?" asked Amanda.

"Because I didn't want you to expect to see her and then wonder where she was. I knew you'd rather cry at home with us. And if something is real, I can't pretend it's not," her mom answered.

"'Died' and 'Amy' just don't seem to go together," said Amanda.

> By addressing your child's fears honestly, you give her real answers that really work.

"I agree. It's so hard to believe," answered Amanda's mom.

"Why did she have to die?" asked Amanda

"Because a very strong bacteria invaded her body, and she couldn't fight it off," she explained.

"But why is there bacteria?" persisted Amanda.

"Because this world is imperfect," said her mom. "I think

good bacteria have gone bad just like other good things turn bad if they aren't used right. The bacteria that attacked Amy are a distortion of good. We have good bacteria in our stomachs that help digest our food. Perhaps the bad bacteria once did something good, but now they destroy."

"Why did God give a tree of good and evil so we'd have a chance to make the world bad?" said Amanda, recalling church lessons about sin. "If He knew we'd mess things up, why did He give us a chance to do it?"

Amanda's mom swallowed uncomfortably, not sure how to answer questions that have troubled theologians for centuries. She then gave it her best shot. "Because He knew we needed the freedom to choose. He must have known the good was somehow worth the pain. It's a hard thing for even grown-ups to understand. What we really mean by 'Why?' is 'Can't we have Amy back?'"

"That's right. I miss her so much, Mom."

Children don't hesitate to ask the questions we grown-ups keep inside. When they ask questions, it shakes us up and reminds us of our own questions. But we've got to answer as best we can. If we don't know, we need to say so, and keep trying to find that answer. Chapter 8 offers some ideas.

EQUIP YOUR CHILD TO MANAGE THE PAIN

Whether or not we understand the reasons for the crises that cause our children pain, we can equip our children to face them. We can show boys and girls what to do. Sarah's frustration over soccer lessened and changed in tone after the second soccer practice.

She lamented, "The coach talks too soft and too fast. I'll never understand him."

"Yes, his voice is hard to understand," I agreed. "Even Daddy and I miss what he says sometimes."

"I'll never understand the coach, and the other girls will," continued Sarah.

"We'll find a way," I assured her.

When Sarah had trouble understanding the coach, I thought seriously about pulling her off the team. As I reviewed her comments over the previous several days, I noticed more statements that indicated she wanted to play than that she didn't want to. Pulling her from the team would teach her that the way to deal with hearing frustrations is to quit. It would reinforce her fear that she might not be able to handle the problems of daily living. It would deprive her of the normal life I feared losing. Instead of pulling her from the team, I equipped her with explanation, with humor, with presence.

We drew pictures of the soccer field and identified the name of each position. I explained what the player in each position does and why. We reviewed until she could teach me. She became excited about the concept of teamwork.

When she worried that she would forget what to do, I reminded her that she doesn't forget other things. I then teasingly said: "What if you forget your name? What if you forget your sister? What if you forget how to walk?"

"Oh, Mom, you are so silly," Sarah said, no longer worried. In her relaxed state I was better able to say, "And if you forget the soccer plays, we'll remind you. That's what practices are for."

I stood close to Sarah during practice. I volunteered to help the coach execute drills. It was natural for me to repeat the coach's instructions, both for Sarah and for the other girls.

After each practice we reviewed what was taught and how to do it.

Equipping can't always come through conversations and advance planning. When two-year-old Mike had emergency stitches, there was no time to talk things through calmly. Instead, his dad held Mike close and whispered words of assurance. As Mike screamed, his dad talked in his ear.

"Yes, it hurts; but it will be over soon. I'm right here next to you to help you through this. Yes, it hurts, but we'll be back home soon. This will help your leg get better. It's almost over. Ouch—that was a tough stitch, wasn't it? Just hold Daddy tight when it hurts. I'm right here. There. Almost finished. We're done."

Young Mike could then collapse in his daddy's arms, the same arms that had given him the strength to handle the stitches. As a toddler, Mike might not express appreciation for his dad's comfort. In fact, he might lash out at his dad for putting him through it. But Mike experienced much less trauma in the arms of his father than all by himself.

Sometimes equipping means suggesting action or helping your child with her own idea. Shortly after Amanda's friend Amy died, Amanda asked, "Mom, will you take me to the store?"

"Why do you want to go?" her mother responded.

"I want to send Carol [Amy's sister] some floss to make friendship bracelets," said Amanda.

Through tears of pride at her sensitivity, her mother responded, "Yes, we'll go first thing in the morning."

Using her own money, Amanda purchased twenty-two

gifts to give to Carol, then wrapped and numbered them. Carol's first three weeks without Amy would hold more joy because of Amanda's care. Amanda felt less desperate because she had done something with her grief.

Love Notes

If you are the friend of a family in crisis, understand the incredible energy it takes just to go on with life. Listen, give encouragement, and help with the daily tasks.

OFFER HOPE WHILE ACCEPTING PRESENT PAIN

No matter how severe the crisis, we Christians can make it through. We make it because there's a better day coming. One day Jesus will return, and there will be no more pain or tears (Rev. 21:4). This hope doesn't take away the pain, but it gives us light to walk toward. After I explained that my daughter Emily had a 70 percent chance of disease-free survival from cancer, my sensitive friend Lynne pointed out, "That's the hope, but the pain is now." She gave me permission to hurt. And I hugged her for it.

Give your children similar permission by letting them feel their pain. When Amanda's friend Amy died, Amanda's sister Susan felt the pain, too.

"I keep trying not to think about Amy's death, but it stays in my brain," said Susan.

"It's OK, honey, just cry and feel," her mother responded.

"I don't want to go to school anymore. I want to see Amy," Susan wailed.

"We'll see her in heaven, but we have to wait until then. I wish we could see her now."

Turning to her sister's pain, Susan asked, "What if Amanda is sad all the time? Or what if Amanda forgets Amy is dead?"

At six years of age, Susan feared that missing someone who could never come back meant you would always be sad. She also thought the opposite was true—if you were happy again, you would forget the person who died. Her parents helped her mesh the two.

"We'll always miss Amy, but we will feel happy again. Sometimes thinking of her will bring smiles to our faces because we'll remember a funny thing she said, or we'll remember a fun thing we did together. Other times thinking of her will make us feel very sad because we wish she were here and could do things with us. Both happy and sad feelings are a sign of love. The strong pain we feel right now won't last forever."

Susan's parents accepted her pain but gave her hope for better times ahead. They used Scripture and experience to verify both the pain and the hope. It's a delicate balance, but one worth striving for.

LET THE FEELINGS GO

Children teach us a lot by the way they experience pain. Especially when they are very young, children express pain fully. They cry or put their sadness into frank words. When the source of pain is gone, so is their worry about it. Sarah seldom lets her frustration over soccer bother her for long. Her anguish is intense when it comes; but after she expresses herself, she attacks new challenges rather than fretting about past ones. She finds ways to hear. She finds ways to make friends. She moves from worry to action. Sarah teaches me to break my adult pattern of worrying about pain before, during, and after it happens. She and other children accept pain, walk through it, and then forget about it.

Perhaps children understand that pain is a part of life—not a fun part, but a definite part. Perhaps they understand Bible writer Peter's admonition, "Dear friends, do not be surprised at the painful trial you are suffering, as though something strange were happening to you" (1 Peter 4:12). But even with this understanding, children's pain matters. Don't minimize it with "they're children; they'll get over it" or similar clichés. Pain is a part of living on this imperfect earth. In heaven we'll have no more pain, but for now we do. Help your children live this reality by accepting their pain, helping them interpret and respond to it, and walking through pain with them. As Christians, we have the added advantage of God's care, company, counsel, and comfort. He'll show us just what to do and how.

Bonus Resources

Music is a fabulous source of feeling expression. One example is *Friends of the Family*—Songs recorded on cassette tape that guide children to accept and express feelings. Available from Celebration Shop, Inc., P.O. Box 355, Bedford, TX 76095. (817) 268-0020. Your medical caregivers can suggest others.

THE POINT ⟵

Children's honesty makes it both easier and more heart-wrenching to encounter crises with them. No matter how agonizing the words, accept your child's feelings and your feelings in order to really heal. Denying feelings or holding them in causes a festering wound. As you accept, express, and respond to feelings, you and your child will find healing and wholeness.

Chapter 2

Walk Through Crises Together

"Two are better than one . . . .
A cord of three strands is not quickly broken."
Ecclesiastes 4:9,12

I crunched myself into position, serving as the pillow for my hunched-over daughter, Emily. Her goal was to make her back as round as possible so the spinal tap needle could enter her spine in the least painful position. She struggled to relax as a huge needle approached her back. With her body around mine, I could complement her relaxed state or talk her into renewed calmness if she became tense.

"Un-way, Oo-tay, Ee-thray," counted Emily's nurse in pig Latin, to distract Emily from the painful procedure. "Ood-gay, irl-gay. It's-ay ipping-dray." The needle was in, and the spinal fluid was dripping on the first try. This

nurse was so skilled. She let Emily know what to expect
and then did each step with speed and precision, all the
while talking in pig Latin to make it easier.

The nurse gave a play-by-play to let Emily know when
the first tube of spinal fluid was full ("ube-tay un-way").
The second ("ube-tay oo-tay"), and finally the third ("ube-
tay ee-thray"). Those three minutes seemed like an eter-
nity. "Ime-tay or-fay the edicine-may," said the nurse to let
Emily know she would hold the needle steady long enough
to insert the medicine to replace the now missing spinal
fluid. While the fluid dripped, the needle had hung loose
and didn't hurt much.
Holding it steady would
increase the pain. The
nurse talked more dur-
ing this time to help
Emily manage it.

> Together—that's the
> key word in parenting
> through crisis.

"The edicine-may is-ay in-ay. The eedle-nay is-ay oming-
cay out-ay. Un-way, oo-tay, ee-thray," said the nurse as she
pulled out the needle.

"You can sit up now," a relieved me told my relieved
daughter. "It's over again for another week."

Together we'd made it through one more in the seem-
ingly endless series of spinal taps, a procedure to verify that
no leukemia cells had entered Emily's central nervous system and to prevent any from going there.

You and your child walk through the crisis together.
Together you can manage the pain, talk through the dread,
and cope with the aftereffects.

God knows how important company is on the scary walk
through pain.

The Bible describes the power of God's company:

"Even though I walk through the valley of the shadow of death, I will fear no evil, for You are with me; Your rod and Your staff, they comfort me" Psalm 23:4.

And the Bible affirms the value of human company:

"Two are better than one... if one falls down, his friend can help him up...if two lie down together, they will keep warm. But how can one keep warm alone? Though one may be overpowered, two can defend themselves. A cord of three strands is not quickly broken" Ecclesiastes 4:9-12.

You Can Run But You Can't Hide

Like our children, we'd like to put off the shot, the stitches, and the painful encounter until another day. But what has to be done has got to be done. All the wishes in the world won't make the bone heal without proper setting and casting. All your anger that your child has to go through continuing pain won't prevent your diabetic child from needing a daily insulin injection. All your fear of needles won't complete the biopsy. Rather than abandon your child to face painful procedures alone, empower your child with your presence. Overcome your own pain by focusing on your child.

Walk through the crisis together, recognizing pain as something you go through, not something you end with. Perhaps that's the first key to managing pain—knowing there's joy on the other side. Some of this joy comes naturally: the joy of the procedure being over, the joy of going back home, the joy of the next activity. You may want to provide other joy yourself: dance a silly jig after each day's insulin shot, decorate the new cast with glow-in-the-dark markers, or meet Dad for lunch after the tedious hearing test. When circumstances permit, talk with your child about what he'd like to do after the hurting is over. Then focus on that joy as you walk through the crisis.

Child's Viewpoint

Children see painful and scary procedures as exactly that—painful and scary. They don't care whether the shot will help them or not. They don't want it because it hurts. Rather than respond with logic, give comfort and presence. Of course, you'll explain that the purpose of the procedure is to help your child get better, but focus on helping him through the experience.

Let's face it. A shot is a shot. Anything with needles is going to hurt. But it can hurt less. There are four basic ways to reduce pain:

• EMLA®
• Speed
• Distraction
• A skillful nurse or doctor

Pray for and seek health-care givers who work well with your child and who do painful procedures quickly, effectively, and relatively painlessly. If your child faces repeated procedures, notice professionals who worked well before and request them next time. This is not the time to defer to medical training needs; instead kindly but firmly request the person your child most trusts and the one who is best at the procedure. Then together with your health-care practitioner, try one or more of these approaches to speed up the process or distract your child from the pain:

- Apply EMLA® to the site of the injection, biopsy, spinal tap, or other procedure. This by-prescription-only cream numbs the site so completely pain is almost eliminated for many procedures. The cream must be applied an hour or more in advance. Insist on this no matter how old your child is or how "simple" the injection. There's no reason to endure unnecessary pain.
- Tell your child about the procedure early enough to let him get ready, but not early enough to prompt undue worry. Some children like to know several hours ahead; others prefer a ten-second warning. My Emily does not want to know the date of her chemotherapy appointment or the procedures that await her until she wakens that day.
- Once your child knows the shot or other painful procedure is coming, do it quickly.
- Hold your child in your lap, put your arms around him, or touch him in whatever way he finds comforting. Whisper calming words.
- Give your child as much control as possible by allowing her to say "3-2-1-Go" or by letting her choose where on the table to sit. While allowing the child to count to three, don't let her delay the procedure through telling one more story, asking to count higher, or running to the rest room. Sometimes the anticipation really is worse than the procedure.
- Teach your child how to relax his body through deep breathing or other relaxation techniques. Let him breathe rapidly to cope with intense parts of the process. These

effective-for-childbirth techniques also work for other pain. The key is knowing how to breathe when. Your nurse will help you and your child know.

- Give your child a pinwheel and challenge her to blow it as fast as it will go. She will pay more attention to this activity than to the shot or procedure.
- Talk through the procedure in pig Latin (ig-pay atin-Lay) or other silly language. Translating the instructions distracts from the pain.
- Take along a wrapped gift to open after the procedure. Squeezing and guessing the gift can both distract your child and make her want to complete the procedure. Rattly, soft, or squeezable presents are especially effective. For continuing crises, keep a box of wrapped gifts and let your child choose one before leaving home. Let friends who ask, "What can I do?" fill this present box.
- During an extended procedure, talk with your child about something he likes. If your son fishes, invite him to tell the nurse about his last fishing trip—what color the water was, how many fish he caught, what the fish looked like, and more. As he talks, he focuses less on the pain.
- Tell stories or play a tape of yourself telling stories. Play the stories through headphones if the procedure is noisy.
- Invite your child to take along a stuffed animal or comforting blanket.
- Explain exactly what will happen if it helps your child to prepare for what's coming. This approach lets her know that it won't hurt unless you warn her first.
- Don't tell what's coming if your child prefers that. One teenager covers his head with a coat and sings a song to himself while he undergoes procedures. He does better when he doesn't know what's coming.

- Let your child play her favorite music and sing or hum along.
- Agree on a treat afterward, such as going out to a specific restaurant, baking cookies, or visiting someone special. Some call this bribery. I call it anticipating the pleasant future.
- Maintain some sense of humor about everything, letting your child take the lead and telling jokes *with* your child rather than *about* him—"Mmmm, this hospital food is the greatest. I can hardly wait to eat it."
- Ask medical professionals for unused syringes (without needles, of course), bandages, anesthesia masks, and other items used in the procedure so the child can play through the process at home. This activity helps him prepare for repeated procedures and work through feelings about a past procedure. Playing helps a child understand what has happened or will happen, express his feelings, and feel in control.

It all boils down to finding what makes your child most comfortable and doing it. Be willing to try something you wouldn't usually do, such as sing a song out loud, to help your child relax. When possible, call ahead to learn details of the procedure, to request health-care givers who are especially good with your child's age and temperament, and to choose the least busy time of day for the procedure. Do whatever works for your child.

Love Notes

Children in medical crises need doctors who will talk with them and treat them as people. They need nurses who can give shots quickly and relatively painlessly with no extra sticks. Children need technicians who can attach the casts and give the x-rays with humor and adventure. Armed with both appreciation and high expectation, find the medical teams who can help your child in these ways. Children are children, not guinea pigs, not miniature adults, not cases. Protect your children from overzealous interns and from being used as learning material for bumbling doctors. Certainly we need to cooperate with teaching hospitals, because experience with our children may save another child's life. But be certain the students are skilled in doing procedures as painlessly as possible. Be certain that promising professionals know how to diagnose and treat accurately. If you are uncertain, tactfully request that an experienced professional accompany the rookie.

EQUIP WITH INFORMATION AND ENCOURAGEMENT

You can't always be with your child. Parents are rarely allowed in the recovery room and even less often in the operating room. You can't go to school with your child, nor can you accompany him through his private thoughts. For circumstances like these, equip your child with information, recommendations, Bible promises, and assurance.

When Lorenzo was scheduled for one-day surgery, his mom found out as much as she could about the procedure. After talking with the doctor, she called the day surgery unit at the hospital and asked to speak with someone who worked in that unit and could explain the policies.

"This is Laura Galindo. My son Lorenzo will have ear tubes inserted Thursday by Dr. Hill. Is this a good time to explain the day surgery process to me?"

"Certainly, what do you want to know?" asked a short-stay nurse.

"We want to know what will happen from the minute we walk in the hospital door until we leave. I'll explain these details to my son so he will know what's coming and will be less apprehensive," said Mrs. Galindo.

"When you first arrive, you'll fill out paperwork. Then, after waiting a short time, Lorenzo will go to a room where he'll give a urine sample and a blood sample. Tell him he can choose his own bandage and the nurses give stickers," said the nurse.

"He'll like that," said Mrs. Galindo.

"Then the two of you will go to the short-stay unit where Lorenzo will have his own room with a television and closet. I, or a member of my staff, will meet you there. You might want to bring a few things to do, because he may have to wait awhile there or wait at some of the previous stops.

"While Lorenzo changes into a hospital gown, I'll ask you more questions. Then we'll take his temperature and blood pressure. About an hour before surgery we'll wheel him to the holding room. You might tell him how fun it is to ride on a rolling bed," suggested the nurse.

Mrs. Galindo thanked the nurse for knowing what

would matter to her small son. She felt safe putting him in her care.

"The anesthesiologist, the surgical nurse, and perhaps the doctor will speak to you in the holding room," continued the nurse. "Following surgery your son will spend about thirty minutes in recovery and then return to you in the short-stay unit."

"How long can we stay with him?" asked Lorenzo's mom.

"You'll be with him until they take him from the holding room to surgery. Then as soon as he wakes up in recovery, we'll bring him to you," said the nurse. "All in all, he'll be away from you about an hour."

"Can he take anything with him into surgery?" asked Mrs. Galindo.

"Certainly. A blanket, a teddy bear, or something else that he likes. Be sure to let the surgical nurse know what he's taking so she can help keep up with it. Sometimes they put a bandage on the doll or teddy bear," added the nurse.

Lorenzo's mom explained these details to Lorenzo. She asked him to let her know what the anesthesia smelled like and to count the people in each room. She then assured Lorenzo that she would be waiting for him after the operation was over and that God would be taking good care of him, even when she couldn't be there.

Lorenzo returned from surgery saying, "Like bubble gum and five. The stuff smelled like bubble gum, and five people were in the last room."

The challenges gave Lorenzo something to focus on besides fear. The information kept him from fearing the unknown. The assurance helped him know that his parent would be nearby and that God would walk with him through every step of surgery.

Nikki faced continual ridicule at the school lunch table. Her dad wanted to march into the cafeteria and knock a couple of heads together, but he knew that wouldn't do. Besides, Nikki wanted to solve the problem herself. They took turns listing possibilities.

- Dad said Nikki could move to another lunch table but Nikki said the other tables were full.
- Nikki wanted to skip lunch to study, but Dad said she needed the break, the nourishment, and the confidence that she didn't have to run from problems.
- Dad suggested Nikki try guiding the conversation by asking questions to get the girls talking about subjects that wouldn't lead to ridicule.
- Nikki thought of ridiculing back, but she didn't want to hurt them or fight fire with fire.
- Dad and Nikki generated reasons the girls said such cruel things—taking their frustrations out on her, expressing jealousy, saying what others said, not knowing what else to talk about. Nikki repeated her commitment to never hurt someone by talking the way they talked to her.
- Nikki said there were other people she'd rather sit with, but she didn't know them well enough yet.
- Dad suggested she try to make friends one by one with other people.

The two decided Nikki would do this last step and watch for open places at other tables. If she got nearer the front of the line, more places might be open. They agreed the problem was not an easy one. Dad continued to listen as Nikki poured out her hurt and anger. He told her how angry it makes him when someone hurts her. They found Matthew 10:19-20 as a reminder of God's care in the lunchroom: "But when they arrest you, do not worry about what to say or how to say it. At that time you will be given what to say, for it will not be you speaking, but the Spirit of your Father speaking through you." Nikki felt better just knowing her dad cared.

Chris worried about his friend Paul. Paul had congenital heart damage. From time to time his heart beat too rapidly, and he became very sick. Every time this happened, Chris feared for Paul's life. But he told no one. Chris's dad asked why Chris had been so quiet, but Chris said nothing. Finally he gave Chris a notebook, saying that he began keeping a journal when he was Chris's age and that Chris might like to write one, too. He explained that a journal is a private book for writing personal thoughts and feelings, and people read a journal only when the writer gives them permission.

Chris kept the journal for a while before writing in it. But one day he brought it to his dad to read. Chris shared his feeling more easily in writing than in conversation. Even when he didn't show his dad his journal, the writing process helped him walk through his fears.

Give

- Tools,
- Information,
- Challenges,
- Ideas,
- Assurance,
- Encouragement both when you can and when you can't be there.

You Can Run and Hide Now

When the surgery, treatment, or trauma is over, you and your child can, and probably should, hide (Matt. 14:23). This retreat gives God an opportunity to heal and refresh you. Your hibernation period can be as brief as a deep breath or as long as a weekend getaway.

Take the time both you and your child need to rest, to heal, and to recuperate. Some parents like to rest with friends; others prefer family time. For deeply traumatic or continuing crises, some families need up to a year or more of reduced activity, mingling daily responsibilities with times for reflection. Discover the way God heals you best.

I try to approach my daughter's chemotherapy logically, reminding myself that she is doing well, that the chemo can whip the cancer once and for all, that three out of four weeks are basically free of side effects, that we can get through the chemo week because we've made it through before. But when my daughter and I return home from a

The intensity of a painful experience exhausts both body and emotions.

day at the cancer clinic, I'm wiped out every time. This chemo visit happens on a Wednesday. On Wednesday nights I teach a youth Bible study class followed by a youth worker meeting. I've tried going on to church on these nights, but I'm too exhausted emotionally to finish my sentences or to stay patient with my active high school group. So I get a substitute ahead of time, and my family huddles together to recover. By the weekend, the chemotherapy side effects are so severe that we miss

Sunday School and church, also. We go off to a motel to concentrate fully on our daughter's needs. We call these trips "adventure weekends," trying to mingle a little joy with the pain. Anticipating the joy helps my daughter— and the rest of the family—through the chemotherapy.

Love Notes

Volunteer to take over for your friend's church or work responsibilities during a crisis. You'll minister in an important way, because your friend cares deeply for the people in her class and the responsibilities at work. She wants to know they're well taken care of in her absence. Because a continuing crisis is not over in the first week or two, ask the dates of return doctor visits and restate your offer to substitute or help in another way.

The children at the pediatric cancer clinic have their own way of retreating. As each child emerges from the treatment room, the waiting room crowd applauds. Then the children start their party. They find all kinds of reasons to celebrate—birthdays, Christmas, Valentine's Day, the end of someone's chemo, cure day, unparty day. Knowing a party awaits makes going to the cancer clinic more fun and makes the aftereffects more bearable.

Helena has discovered a post-chemotherapy retreat that works uniquely for her. Her medicines make her too nauseated to party afterward, so she and a friend do something fun the night before. They stay up really late so she'll be sleepy on chemo day. Her mom gasses up the car before arriving at the hospital. Then as soon as chemo is over, Helena crawls in the backseat and sleeps while her mom drives the four hours to their home. As long as the car is moving, Helena stays asleep and she doesn't vomit. These four hours of respite get her ready for a long night with the commode.

Love Notes

Discover how your friend likes to recover after a painful experience. Give her your presence and a listening ear if she wants company. Give her privacy and protection if she needs to be alone with her family. In both cases, meet continuing needs by arranging ahead of time to bring a meal (in disposable containers), by doing laundry, by leaving voicemail or email messages, or by offering to care for other children.

After Barbara's youngest daughter died, Barbara said, "My soul went into hibernation. It was alive but not active. I could have denied the pain, in which case God could never have healed me. I could have rejected my faith, which would have left me nowhere to turn. Or I could go through the pain knowing that I would hold on to my faith and my joy. I've taken this last approach. It may be the most painful of the three initially, but it has given me the foundation I need to survive as a whole and happy person. Walking through my grief was the only way to heal and to care for my other two children."

Barbara's tiny bit of hope during the darkness has sustained her. During her time of retreat she needed steady care; plenty of time to simply be; friends who would listen; and confidence that, though she could not feel it, the joy would return to her life.

Wise Barbara recognized that pain, grief, and suffering are not contrary to Christianity. They're a recognition that people matter. Sadly, rather than friends who understood this, Barbara encountered Christians who tried to explain away her pain with trite phrases like, "God won't put you through more than you can bear," and "At least it's not worse." They misquoted 1 Corinthians 10:13, a verse about temptation, not suffering. Impatient for her to get on with life, they added to Barbara's burden rather than helped her carry it (Gal. 6:2).

One friend understood her need to heal. This friend spent countless hours with Barbara, listening to her, hugging her, getting her out of the house, and helping her with daily chores. She talked with Barbara's children, asking them about school and the other events in their lives. This friend's actions showed confidence that God would heal Barbara.

"We don't have to be super-happy people to express our faith," explained Barbara. "As I healed, I needed to think and feel. At first I couldn't even do that. My friend understood this."

Let people love you well, both during and after your retreat. My favorite source of support is not an organized group or a professional caregiver, but my mother-in-law, with whom I've already shared both happy and sad times. She checks with our family, listens, empathizes. She hurts along with us, achieving that delicate balance between becoming overemotional and distancing herself from the pain. She invites us to her home for weekend getaways, caring for the children while my husband and I rest both physically and emotionally. She takes care of us, giving us mother-love in just the way we need it, making us feel safe and at home.

Debbie's friend treated her similarly. As Debbie and her son walked into church for the first time after his cancer diagnosis, a sensitive friend met her at the door and said, "This day will be hard for you, won't it? I just want you to know I'm praying." Her encouraging words brought tears to Debbie's eyes but also empowered her. As hard as it was to go on with life, Debbie knew she had to, for her son's sake and for her own. To do otherwise was to let the cancer and the chemotherapy steal the very life Debbie feared losing. Debbie's friend reminded her that life is worth returning to.

> Pain, grief, and suffering are not contrary to Christianity. They're a recognition that people matter.

Take your retreat from the pain. Then let those retreats become a part of your life, not a replacement for it. Let your grief and your joy commingle in an unnatural, but effective, mix. Go on with life, confident that God will empower you and your child to face the challenges ahead, and confident that joy does come in the morning (Psalm 30:5).

THE POINT ←

As you parent your child through crisis, go through it together. Let nothing, even your own fears, keep you from your child's side during a medical emergency, an illness, or some other physical pain. When the crisis occurs at school or a location where you cannot go, offer your constant support and equip your child with specific skills to manage the crisis.

Chapter 3

Equip to Participate Fully in Life

"Finally, be strong in the Lord and in His mighty power. Put on the full armor of God so that you can take your stand against the devil's schemes. . . . Stand firm then, with the belt of truth buckled around your waist, with the breastplate of righteousness in place, and with your feet fitted with the readiness that comes from the gospel of peace."
Ephesians 6:10-11,14-15

People really don't understand handicapped children," lamented Mr. Randolf. "Greg has all kinds of problems at school because people avoid him, pick him last for teams, and accuse him of being dumb. He's not dumb or slow in sports. He just can't see well enough to work faster," Mr. Randolf continued. "People don't want anything to do with him. He comes home discouraged, lonely, and sad."

"Have you been to talk to the class, to help them understand Greg's poor vision and what he's capable of?" asked Mr. Lupo, the Randolfs' next-door neighbor.

"No. I don't want to make a big deal of it," said Mr. Randolf.

"Well, have you helped Greg learn ways to make and keep friends by working around his vision problems?" Mr. Lupo prodded.

"As far as Greg's concerned, there is no problem. He says he sees just fine. We don't really talk about it," said Mr. Randolf.

"I like his positive outlook. But if you don't equip Greg or his classmates, they can't move past the vision obstacle," said Mr. Lupo.

"I don't want people to focus on Greg's poor vision," objected Mr. Randolf.

"Our experience has been that a little attention does just the opposite. Explaining things enables peers and teachers to turn their focus away from the vision problem," said Mr. Lupo. "When Greg, his friends, and his teachers understand what's going on with Greg's eyes, they can move past their curiosity and discomfort to become genuine friends."

"Yeah, but then people will tease," insisted Mr. Randolf.

"People tease when they don't understand," explained Mr. Lupo. "When Aurelio had that long hospitalization and recovery period, the doctor gave me information to share with his schoolmates. I got permission from the principal and teacher to talk with the class. I shared the tips in a little rhyme and then answered questions. We haven't had any teasing or cruelty, except from kids in other classes."

"I know; I know. But your situation is different," said Mr. Randolf. "I just want people to understand. Because things are hard for Greg, he's moody and demanding. People just have to see that."

Greg's biggest problem is not his physical handicap. It's a dad who spoils him. He and his dad are in need of a little life-goes-on training. Rather than moving on with life, they want to make exceptions for him. Rather than understanding, they want excuses. Mr. Randolf wants people to tiptoe around Greg's difficulties and to condone his self-centered behavior. This is neither realistic nor fair to Greg. By refusing to equip Greg and his friends to manage the vision difficulties, Mr. Randolf is unwittingly handicapping Greg even more severely. The ability to make and keep friends is well within Greg's reach. His eyes are messed up, not his friendship capacity.

By trying to hide the difficulty and by pampering his son, Mr. Randolf creates in Greg the expectation that people owe him attention. This makes Greg a spoiled and demanding person, a person others avoid even when he sees perfectly. Greg and Mr. Randolf may blame his friendship problems on his eyesight, but these problems are a product of self-centeredness, a handicap no one has to have.

Greg needs to move on with life, and Greg needs his dad to equip him to do so. Moving on with life is more than just deciding to grin and bear it. It's grabbing the rays of joy that burst through pinholes in the pain. It's developing techniques and attitudes that enable your child to do his best in spite of the handicap or sadness. It's finding ways to carry the burden or walk around the obstacles. It's confidence that God's power is big enough to manage anything.

Bonus Resources

Children share their stories of moving on with life in *How It Feels to Fight for Your Life* (Little, Brown and Company, 1989) and *How It Feels to Live with a Physical Disability* (Simon and Schuster, 1992) by Jill Krementz.

FIND WAYS AROUND THE ROADBLOCK

Moving on with life begins by recognizing that crises are interruptions to life, not the end of life. They're a part, not the whole. Greg's vision problems are major, but Greg still has a brilliant brain, a big heart, two working arms, and two strong legs. Certainly his vision problems get in the way, but he can detour around them. He can find and keep friends, discover and excel at talents, challenge and master school, cooperate with and stay an integral part of his family. With the guidance of his parents and other caring adults, he can be as happy and fulfilled as any other child. Going on with daily routines can give Greg the success, friendship, and experiences that make life worth living. But Greg's dad blocked Greg from all of this.

As Aurelio's dad, Mr. Lupo, has discovered, these good things happen when we equip our children to work around their crises, not when we expect others to threat them differently. Children in crisis are children first and, like all children, they have the capacity to care for others, to succeed, and to enjoy life. Like all children, they must learn the skills that don't come naturally for anyone—sensitivity, considerateness, kindness, and cooperativeness. They must learn to try without fear, to fail without pouting, to succeed without bragging. They must learn to study, remember, understand, use information, and master school. They must learn to express emotions calmly, generate solutions, channel anger, and solve problems directly rather than pity themselves. These skills may be more difficult for challenged children, but they are all the more crucial.

My Sarah's hearing loss makes it difficult for her to follow a group conversation in a noisy room. Cafeteria chatter or large family gatherings are especially frustrating. She initially attacked this problem by calling for everyone's attention when she started to speak. One-sided conversations aren't much fun for anyone, including Sarah. So Sarah is learning to watch one or two people at a time, to get the gist of the conversation, and to ask questions that encourage others to talk. She contributes to the connected conversation rather than adds isolated stories.

> Moving on with life is more than just deciding to grin and bear it. It's grabbing the rays of joy that burst through pinholes in the pain.

Conversation by grueling conversation, she's growing skills for overcoming her hearing obstacle. Learning to listen to others requires much more effort than controlling the conversation, but it makes Sarah a more enjoyable dinner partner and a better friend.

Equipping your child takes more initial work than indulging him. But in the long run it saves work and misery. Every time I watch Sarah struggle to follow the conversation, my mama-heart breaks. I want to shout, "Give her a chance!" But my mama-heart is equally convinced that she can clear this hurdle. She can participate in meaningful and life-changing conversation. It may never be easy, but she will experience success. Every child finds competence and confidence when equipped with life skills. Let your child's happiness become your motivation to prod good behavior rather than pity his sad circumstance, to teach him coping skills rather than expect people to cope with him.

Love Notes

As you move on with life, avoid the "special" label. "Special is a new pair of shoes, not a handicap or a problem," said a wise teacher of preschoolers. Let your actions show that your child in crisis is more like other children than different. Work to keep your child's daily experiences as normal as possible, rejoicing when she faces the same problems every other child complains about. Let her be a child who just happens to have leg braces, not the kid with the leg braces.

RETURN TO ROUTINE

Obviously, moving on with life after a crisis doesn't mean you insist that your child be immediately competent or that he keep the stiff upper lip at all times. Following the accident that injured his eyes, Greg needed time to recover physically and to grieve over his loss. He needed time to cry, to wish for his vision back, to feel sorry for himself. But as soon as physically able, he should return to school and readjust to routine. Going on with daily routine can be excruciating; but it can also give the success, friendship, and experiences that make life worth living. As Greg and his family move on with life, their sadness over his loss of vision can coexist with the happiness of ordinary life. The mix is not always comfortable, but it is effective. And it is much tastier than a steady diet of sadness.

Day by uncertain day, Aurelio's parents discovered the crisis-coping value of routine life. After a two-week hospitalization, Aurelio balked at returning to school. Careful listening revealed several reasons for his reluctance, including fear that he wouldn't know the answers or that things might have changed since he had been there last. Aurelio feared making a mistake or looking stupid.

These fears surprised Mr. and Mrs. Lupo, since Aurelio is a very strong student. But rather than say, "But you're too smart for that!" they took his fears seriously. They knew Aurelio's homebound teacher could continue to teach him the material, but they also knew Aurelio needed the confidence and connectedness that would come from returning to school and friends. Prodded by the doctor's orders, they sent him on to school that first day. They armed him with the assurance that it might take a little time, but he would soon feel a part of school again. They felt cruel pushing their still weak child into the "big bad school" and spent an anxious day worrying over whether they had done the right thing.

When Aurelio came home happy, his parents breathed sighs of relief. The problem recurred the second day.

Aurelio said he didn't feel quite good enough to go. They again pushed him on, urging him to try half a day. He stayed a full day. The third day he came home sad because he'd missed a question in the math game. His parents reminded him that he had missed that skill while out, and they reviewed it with him at home. After several days and a bit of troubleshooting, Aurelio was contentedly back in the school routine.

Shortly afterward, Aurelio had to return to the hospital. His resistance to school began again, and his parents again pushed him on. Every time Aurelio had a problem at school, came home unhappy, or got tired, his parents wondered if sending him to school was the right thing to do. Sending Aurelio on to school day after day was almost harder for Aurelio's parents than for Aurelio. But school helped Aurelio focus more on normal life than on his chronic illness. Aurelio's parents knew they'd done the right thing when, at the end of the year, Aurelio's teachers gave him a courage award for managing both school and his illness so well.

For Aurelio, the alternative to routine school life was studying at home. Though this is required in some cases, staying home could make Aurelio feel and act like an invalid rather than the normal nine-year-old he is. Staying home could have deepened his feelings of alienation, increased his fear of returning to school, and caused him to withdraw from friends. Going on to school took Aurelio's mind off his physical discomforts and gave him something positive to focus on. As a fully functioning student, Aurelio gained confidence, competence, and leadership skills he could gain no other way.

Love Notes

If your child must stay home because of low blood counts, decreased immunity, long recovery, or another unavoidable condition, take action to keep him in touch with friends and routine. Invite friends over if permitted, place a tape recorder in his classroom so he can hear school instruction and conversation, consider a computer link, send videotapes or letters back and forth, attend occasional field trips and programs, or do whatever you can to keep him close to church, school, and other groups that matter.

EQUIP WITH THE SKILLS HE NEEDS

Going on with life means more than just moving on. It means providing the tools, skill training, and practice needed to do so. Alex's moderate hearing loss means he hears well with hearing aids as long as the one talking is within three feet and there are no competing noises such as chairs moving, papers rattling, or music playing. Unfortunately, there are very few situations that meet these criteria. So Alex's parents help him find ways to hear even in less-than-perfect settings. To equip him to hear in his public school classroom, they put tennis balls on the chair legs to silence chair noise and arrange for use of an FM system, a radio-like device that projects the teacher's voice directly to Alex's hearing aid. They encourage Alex to make the most of lip-reading and to ask for clarification when he needs it.

Alex's parents also guide Alex to develop skills that have nothing to do with hearing, such as friendship and problem-solving. They insist that he show thoughtfulness to his friends, that he do his best both at school and at home, and that he solve his problems calmly. When hearing frustrations occur, as they inevitably do, Alex's parents take them seriously and suggest actions that might alleviate the problem. They call on speech teachers and audiologists for tips to solve dilemmas, persisting until his parents find a solution that works. They assure Alex that he can find ways to understand and that they will be there to help him.

When Alex is sad about his hearing loss, his parents listen and cry along, looking past their aching hearts to be grateful he's open with his feelings. Together they yell at the broken ears that refuse to work right. They look forward to heaven, where Alex will hear clearly, and vow not to let the hearing loss take away their joy.

"I still have my family, my friendships, my silliness, and my good brain. My broken ears can't take away those good things," says Alex.

Rather than call Alex "special," his parents say his ears don't work. His hearing difficulties are a fact of life, but they aren't the only fact. He has a clear brain that helps him learn well, a caring spirit that feels his friends' pain, and a spunky personality that finds fun in every circumstance. Alex works as hard to develop these as he does his hearing skills.

Alex's mother shares, "I admit that I inwardly balked against putting hearing aids in my tiny baby's ears. I didn't want him looking funny, and I became frustrated at the number of times he pulled them off and threw them across the room. But I had to move past my self-consciousness to give Alex the hearing devices that would enable him to hear well enough to learn to talk. We even tied the hearing aids to his T-shirt with clear fishing line.

"Today both Alex and I hate the bulky weight of his FM system. We admit our dislike for the thing and our frustration that no one seems interested in making a more compact model. But we move past these feelings to wear it anyway. If we refuse to use hearing aids and FM system, we set Alex up for daily hearing frustration and for missing part of what the teacher says. Refusing to take advantage of tools that give him good hearing would deny him a full life. Only his ears are broken. I know he can accomplish anything he sets his mind to do. I must simply help him find the ways."

Stan copes with Williams syndrome, a congenital abnormality that causes physical limitations and mild mental retardation. Stan's continuing chatter and amiable ways endear him to teachers and peers. Because things are difficult for Stan, he frequently asks teachers or friends to do physical tasks or academic assignments for him. He especially targets substitute teachers.

"Won't you pick up that ball for me, Mrs. Myers?"

Wise Mrs. Myers responded, "Stan, I know you can do it!"

"Oh, but it's hard for me to bend that far," said Stan.

"I agree, and it would be hard for me too. I also know you'll feel better if you do it yourself," said Mrs. Myers.

"Doggone! Who'd you hear that from? Now I'll have to do all my own work today," said Stan with a grin.

Stan's parents equip Stan to do his own work by warning teachers not to do for Stan what Stan can do for himself. They want him to achieve just a little more that he did the day before. They also remind Stan that he can do it, that they have confidence in him, and that they're proud when he accomplishes something new. They celebrate each new step. They work to build confidence as well as competence.

Giving Stan unneeded help would keep Stan from developing skills, could lead to Stan's using people, and could decrease Stan's confidence. Stan balks when he's caught trying to get out of work, but he is inwardly glad that someone cares enough to believe in him.

After Leland broke his leg, his parents equipped him to get to class by buying him a comfortable backpack to carry his books. Friends opened doors for him, but Leland carried his own stuff. This approach helped Leland maintain self-sufficiency. Forcing Leland to depend on friends could have given him a weakling image, both in his eyes and in the eyes of his friends. This image could have persisted long after Leland's cast was removed.

See chapter 7 for more ideas on equipping for school.

Child's Viewpoint

Children may initially like the attention that comes from being in a short-term or continuing crisis, but ultimately they don't want to be treated any differently than anyone else. You serve both your child's and your own best interests when you discipline, equip, and guide your child toward a happy and loving personality.

DISCIPLINE AS USUAL

One of the greatest temptations in walking with children through crises is the temptation to spoil them, to treat them differently. We feel badly that they have to go through tough times, so we try to make it easier on them. The catch is this: spoiling makes it harder, not easier.

Hal's mom hoped for a safer and happier Hal when she warned his brothers, "You know how dangerous it is for Hal's heart to beat fast, so if he gets upset, just give in. He's only three, you know." What Hal's mom got was resentful brothers and a spoiled Hal who learned that getting upset meant getting his way. Instead of staying calm, Hal's outbursts increased, putting his heart in even greater danger. He became demanding and stubborn. People dreaded having him in class.

> True love sets consistent limits and gives loving instruction.

What went wrong? Hal learned to control rather than to cooperate. Hal felt like an exception to the family rather than a part of it. Hal learned to manipulate rather than to love. Hal assumed his needs were more important than everyone else's. Hal's family spoiled him rather than loved him.

Hal's not a bad kid. He's normal. Like all normal kids, he needs to learn how to turn outside himself, how to love rather than manipulate. This learning is the purpose of discipline. It's the purpose of parenting. Spoiling is not letting kids have it easy; it's withholding love; it's refusing to offer guidance. True love sets consistent limits and gives loving instruction. Hal needs hugs, encouragement, and affirmation. But these must be coupled with the discipline that guides him to love in return.

Discipline is especially important for children who struggle with crises, because they need extra reserves upon which to draw. When Keith misses his absent dad, he must work extra hard to let his anger out in constructive ways. When Shelly feels tired after a difficult tutoring session, she needs the motivation to say so instead of throwing a tantrum. When Vera is upset over her amputated leg, she must know how to voice her feelings kindly rather than snap at family members or friends.

Think through what you're teaching when you choose a plan of action. Hal's mom taught that it's OK to get your own way if you're sick. Greg's dad taught that a handicap means preferential treatment. Aurelio's parents taught that Aurelio could move beyond his pain to find and create everyday happiness.

> I expect kindness whether they are rested or tired, delighted or frustrated, successful or defeated.

Obviously, the third choice, though initially harder, led to a happier child.

When Alex's parents allow him to get away with a messy room because he didn't hear the instructions to pick it up, they guide him to believe he doesn't have to follow rules. He then expects exceptions to other rules, including the ones God proclaims. If Alex can't learn to consistently obey his parents, he can't learn to obey God. For Alex's sake, his parents must insist he hear them by moving close enough that he can hear, or by awaiting a response after they talk to him. They must make sure he takes responsibility to ask for clarification if he does not understand. They can't accept, "I didn't hear you." They've got to equip him to hear instead.

Sound harsh? It can be if you do it with a waiting-to-catch-you-doing-wrong attitude. But true discipline includes a loving tone along with consistent expectations. It provides skills, not sympathy.

EXPECT THE BEST AND THEN EQUIP THEM TO DO IT

We automatically take care of our children's physical needs, providing wheelchairs if legs don't work, glasses if eyes are weak, and ideas if the previous solution failed. Just as important are the self-discipline skills to manage the responsibility, anger, frustration, relationship problems, and other challenges encountered in daily life.

Begin with strong expectations and then equip your children to meet them. Story after story documents children who have surpassed medical expectations, simply because a parent believed in them and equipped them. Children blossom when given high expectations coupled with the skills to meet them.

One of my strongest expectations is that my children speak with loving words. I expect kindness whether they are rested or tired, delighted or frustrated, successful or defeated. When my Emily feels rotten from chemotherapy's side effects, I must insist, "I know you feel lousy, but you still have to be kind." If I allow her to take her frustrations out on her sister, I teach that kindness is important only when we feel like it. I allow the pain to overcome the joy.

I must guide both of my daughters to overcome their physical pain to show love to others. This does not mean they must be giddy all the time, nor does it mean they must be around people all the time. Instead it means they say, "I just don't feel like talking right now," rather than, "Get out of my face!"

It means they say, "I'd like some privacy right now," rather than, "Quit bugging me!"

Loving words and loving actions are a big order for any person, but they're central to happiness. When we parents guide our children to show Christlike love, we give them crisis coping skills as well as life-enjoying skills. Remembering that true discipline means guidance, I guide my children to meet my expectation for loving words in these W.A.Y.S.:

W.ords to use—I don't just say, "Be kind." I help them modify their words with specific suggestions, just as God does for us (Col. 3:12ff). "Try, 'I'd really like you to understand my point of view on this,' instead of, 'Accept someone else's opinion for a change!' "

A.ffirm the good I hear—Too often we parents focus so hard on correcting our children's shortcomings that we fail to notice their strengths. If I don't balance my corrections with compliments, I'll exasperate and defeat my children (Eph. 6:4). When I compliment my children's kind words and actions, I show that I believe in them, that I recognize their capacity to be kind, and that I'm proud of them. Children discover that they can monitor their own words and attitudes. Consequently, they choose to be caring. Feeling kind makes it easier to be kind.

Y.ou'd feel? In keeping with my view that good discipline leads to self-discipline, I encourage my children to use words they'd like to hear. I ask them to think how their words, actions, or attitudes would make them feel before saying, doing, or expressing them. I try to grow compassion (Heb. 10:24).

S.omething good with the bad. When my children are angry, are hurt, or have a complaint, I encourage them to say something good along with the bad (Eph. 4:29). This may mean beginning with the good, as in: "You're important to me . . ." along with, "so I'm sad that you've been avoiding me lately. What's wrong?" Or it may mean closing with the good, such as: "My back is really aching from the car accident . . ." along with, " . . . but at least I can walk more comfortably."

Recognize discipline as a path to joy, not a stifler of it. Too often we see discipline as punishment, something to be avoided, something too hard for children. But true discipline teaches children how to relate lovingly to other people. Such love is something we all want and need.

> Recognize discipline as a path to joy, not a stifler of it.

Good discipline teaches children how to create lasting closeness. It guides children to care for God, for one another, and for themselves. It brings true freedom and true happiness. True discipline is love and attention coupled with a firm expectation to do what is right.

SEE THE JOY

Going on with life is more than informing, equipping, encouraging, motivating, and disciplining. It's enjoying. God refuses to let the pain of this world push out the joy. He pokes joy into the darkest of darks. Notice and cherish these gifts.

Sarah, pleased about an Easter gift her adult friend Diane had given her, made Diane a candle. On a tiny, egg-shaped candle, Sarah meticulously sculpted a wax picture of Diane and herself. Attaching bits of colored wax, she reproduced the love she felt for her caring friend. She wrapped it carefully and presented it.

"It's so small and so right!" responded Diane. "You can see me looking down at you and you looking up at me. And there's a heart in the middle! You make me so happy, Sarah!"

Both Sarah and Diane were ecstatic. Hearing loss could not get in the way of this precious experience.

Giving and receiving love. Responding to the people in our world. Noticing the good God gives. That's what life is all about. And that's why we go on with life.

THE POINT ←—

Going on with life is more than just plowing ahead. It's insisting that the pain is not the only factor in life, that there is good to be found and enjoyed. It's providing the skills, insight, strategies, self-discipline, and dependence on God that give our children the opportunity to enjoy life fully no matter what the obstacles. We go on not simply because we want to, but because we really can—God lives on, and we can too!

Chapter 4

Invite Friends
to Help

*"People don't understand why you go on
with life, how hard that is to do,
and why it's so important to do so."*
—Gail Linam

I trembled as I entered my youth Sunday School department for the first time after Emily had been diagnosed
with leukemia. I planned to talk with my students about
the diagnosis and what it meant to our family.

A few of my students tend toward rowdiness, and I
feared they would laugh or make wisecracks. I had tried to
anticipate what I'd do if they said anything smart-alecky
but had no answer. As I began to speak, writing down key
details on a large poster, I was overwhelmed by my students' sensitivity. They were silent and attentive. The only
sound was gentle sniffing as they cried along with me.

I wrote the word "WHAT?" and shared the details of diagnosis, the nature of the cancer, and the painful treatments we faced over the next two years. I shared what we'd already been through. Tears began to course down my cheeks, but I took deep breaths and continued, determined to finish.

I wrote the word "WHY?" and explained, "One thing I know about this illness is that it does not come from God. God is the giver of good gifts. Satan is the bringer of evil." I jotted down Matthew 7:9-11 and James 1:13,16-17 and invited volunteers to read them. I said, "This cancer is an imperfect part of this imperfect world. As Matthew 5:45 explains, the rain falls on the good and bad alike. Being a Christian doesn't protect us from tragedy. It gives us power to manage it. Just as I am certain that God didn't do this, I am certain that He won't let it steal our joy. We'll lose energy, and I won't always be able to be here for Sunday School or Wednesday night Bible studies, but somehow God will poke joy into the darkness. We will make it because God is with us."

I wrote the word "HOW?" and jotted down 1 Peter 4:12-19. I read, "Dear friends, do not be surprised at the painful trial you are suffering, as though something strange were happening to you." Then I explained, "Problems are a part of life. I certainly don't like this one, but it's here; and we've got to move on through it. As verse 19 says, we're continuing our commitment to our faithful Creator and we'll continue to do good.

"I'd like your help with this," I added. "I'll be weak over the next months, and I'll need your loving. My family will, too. Hug me when you see me. Don't worry about saying anything; just love me. Rather than be afraid of us or our pain, talk to us like usual. Let us know you're glad to see us. If you feel like it, buy a little something for Emily and her sister and wrap it up—we need surprises for treatment days to open after the shots are over. Most of all, please be good to each other. We need the kind of warm and happy church family that makes us all feel loved as we go through problems."

I invited questions and was amazed at their concern. I wanted to hug them for their genuine care—so I did.

My youth friends didn't just hurt *for* me, they hurt *with* me. When I shared a similar presentation with my Wednesday night youth Bible study group, one six-foot-tall new-to-church sophomore stood and pounded the wall. "I want to fight it, but I don't know how!" I was touched by his unique expression of love. Most would say kids don't care. I'm convinced they do. I shared my appreciation by agreeing that it is a fight, a fight against a disease that God hates even more than we do.

A senior girl slipped me $20 after the meeting. Over my resistance, she insisted I use it to buy medicine for Emily.

The youth cared in the ways they knew, ways we adults have forgotten. As the weeks unfolded the teenagers found more ways to care. A macho-on-the-surface guy did a school paper on chemotherapy and reported to me his irrefutable conclusion that nobody should have to go through that. I agreed. That same fellow sent me a card he had personally chosen and purchased, the only card I received from a teenager. A younger teenager whom I had never met heard about Emily's cancer through a friend. She wrote a paper on leukemia and brought it to me to read. A ninth-grader committed her life to becoming an oncologist so she could whip cancer. Still another found Emily a special book and markers with which to personalize it.

The youth cared quietly but definitely. Some expressions of care surfaced as late as two years later. I wonder how many more cared silently. These teenagers showed me more care than I though possible from even the most mature adults. Even now, I realize with grateful tears that they never would have expressed their care if I hadn't taken the risk to share my pain with them.

SOME WON'T UNDERSTAND

Not all friends are as sensitive as these teenagers. Two months into my daughter's twenty-six month course of chemotherapy, a well-meaning friend asked, "How's Emily?"

"Well, she's entered remission and has passed the worst stage of chemo. We're very thankful for that. Now she's in the second stage, which includes weekly spinal taps and continuous hair loss. We dread the pain of these months," I explained.

"But she's doing well, isn't she?" asked my friend.

"Yes, if you mean she's still in remission," I responded.

"Good. I'm glad. Then basically it's over, right?" my friend persisted.

"No. We have two more years of painful treatment and five years of watchful waiting after that," I said. "And the current side effects are very distressing."

"But she's going to be just fine, isn't she?" he said. And then without waiting for me to respond, he added, "I just know she is."

Once we go on with life, people assume the pain is over. Two weeks is the maximum most friends allow for a crisis.

These friends, both Christians and non-Christians, want the pain to be over both for your sake and for theirs. They don't want you to hurt. But more basically, they don't want to hurt. They want you to be cheerful so they won't have to wrestle with why sad things happen to Christian people. If you're happy in the midst of pain, then maybe the pain's really not that bad, and they won't have to sort it out.

Continuing pain, especially in children, is something many people are unwilling to face. Some try to explain it away; others simply stay away. Either consciously or unconsciously, they think if they ignore the pain, it will go away. Or they try to "blessing-ize" it with holy-sounding words that have nothing to do with what the Bible really says.

> Two weeks is the maximum most friends allow for a crisis.

What makes friends and family members wish instead of help, explain away instead of walk with us through the pain? Is it because they can't handle it? Not at all. God has promised the power (Phil. 4:13). People avoid pain because they choose not to face it. Like ostriches, some people prefer to stick their heads in the sand and pretend that everything is OK.

This would be great if it worked. If wishing and hoping and praying made everything OK, we'd all do it. But all the wishing in the world won't take away the steady pain that comes with rheumatoid arthritis. All the hope we can muster won't bring a beloved grandparent back from the grave. All the skillful praying in powerful churches won't restore a cancerous leg that has been amputated.

Wishes do give us something to work for. Hope does keep our eyes on the perfection God has promised in heaven. Prayers do link us with the source of Power who equips us to face the challenges of a continuing crisis. But we also need loving friends and specific actions to guide our children successfully through crises.

The good news is that these loving friends are there. Like my youth friends, they're waiting in the wings to show you their love. Some care naturally. Others need to be shown what you need. Limit your contact with those who wish away the pain or who "help" in destructive ways. Instead, notice and draw near to the friends who care with the genuine love of Christ.

Find friends and family members who offer practical help, who aren't afraid of a continuing crisis, who love you and your child just as you are, who listen, who respond, who encourage growth toward goodness. Call on friends and family who revive your energy rather than drain it.

At your time of crisis, friends whom you scarcely knew before will come out of the woodwork; others you thought you could count on will fail you miserably. Walk on past the frustration of this.

It takes a big friend to hurt along, to share your tears, to recognize and care about your family's needs, to prod you on to normalcy without forgetting the struggles. Often children are better at this than adults. Recognize and cherish the friends God sends your way. Then work together with them to meet your child's needs.

BEGIN WITH YOUR CHILD'S PEERS

"Jordan has Down's syndrome, which means he learns a little more slowly. He can participate in every activity here at church, and he has the same feelings you do," explained Jordan's mom to a fellow three-year-old. "Could he sit with you this morning until he gets to know the other children a little better?"

These three brief sentences bridged a new friendship for Jordan at church. Jordan's mom recognized her role not only to receive the love of friends but also to build new roads for friendship.

Like Jordan's mom, we parents interpret our children's crises to the rest of the people in their world. This happens both casually and in formal presentations. To do well at this job, we must educate ourselves and our children, inform our children's peers and adult caregivers, enhance the good, and buffer the bad.

The responsibility to educate is both a blessing and a burden. It's a blessing because we know our child best, we know the impact of the crisis, and we know how we want people to respond to it. It's a burden when we're so weary with other demands that we yearn for someone to help us bear the load.

That's the time to take one step at a time. Talk to one person or group at a time, choosing the times most advantageous to your child. Isaiah 40:31 explains that sometimes we'll feel like soaring, other times we can run, and sometimes we simply put one foot in front of the other. No matter how slowly we move, we can move forward, and each step is a step of faith.

To be the valuable friend a parent in crisis is looking for:

DON'T	DO
Avoid me because you feel bad about what has happened.	Tell me how bad you feel so we can share the pain. I like knowing you care enough to hurt with me.
Stay away simply because you don't know what to say.	Give me a hug. It communicates as well as words.
Say, "Call if you need anything."	Say, "I'm free on Tuesday afternoon and am giving you that time. What can I do?" Offer to clean my house, do laundry at your house or mine, prepare a favorite family recipe, or fulfill another daily obligation I haven't the time or energy to do.
Stay a long time when my child is in the hospital.	Bring a smile and a can-do-in-the-hospital toy. Stay only a few minutes. There are exceptions to this—ask how long a visit we need and what we'd like to do while you're here.

DON'T	DO
Talk only to me.	Talk with my child and hear his stories. Offer to play a game with him, visit his room, or see something he made.
Fear feeling, or try to "be strong" for me.	Weep with me and laugh with me (Rom. 12:15). It's so hard to find someone who will cry with me.
Expect me to feel a certain way.	Just let me feel how I feel. I may be ecstatic one day, discouraged the next.
Drop by unannounced.	Call to let me know you're coming so I can let you know if it's a good time.
Forget us.	Remember that long-term crises need continuing care. Write dates such as check-ups or milestones on your calendar. Send cards of encouragement to arrive near those dates. Call ahead of time to find out what care we or our children need.

To be the valuable friend a parent in crisis is looking for:

DON'T	**DO**
Assume a visit is the only way to care.	Send helium balloons. Make or buy cards that tell us how you feel about us. Leave messages on our answering machine. Place surprises at our back door that we'll find when we return from an appointment. Generate a computer banner for our child's room. Send email messages or online cards. Bring fun note papers, interesting bubble baths, tub toys, or tiny trucks. Deliver a child's activity box or a set of parent coupons ("Good for five loads of laundry," etc.). Think of things that show love even when we're too occupied or weary to respond.
Ignore my healthy children.	Bring something for healthy siblings if you bring something for my ill or injured child. Talk to them. Arrange with me to take them places.

DON'T	DO
Force me to talk.	Let me talk when I need to.
Stare at or avoid looking at my child's hair loss, hearing aids, scar, or other physical challenge.	Ask questions about it so we can both understand. Make her feel pretty and capable with sincere compliments that are both related and unrelated to the physical situation.
Call me a hero or think of me as a hero.	Minister to me rather than ask me to buoy you. Accept the pain as an attack against God rather than a gift from Him. Then feel along with me rather than call my pain a merit badge or opportunity for heroism.
Say, "I know how you feel."	Say, "Tell me about it." Then really listen.

He gives strength to the weary
And increases the power of the weak.
Even youths grow tired and weary,
And young men stumble and fall;
But those who hope in the Lord
Will renew their strength.
They will soar on wings like eagles;
They will run and not grow weary,
They will walk and not be faint.
Isaiah 40:29-31

We can refuse the responsibility to educate and take our chances with how people respond. Or we can embrace the responsibility, confident that good interpretive work will prevent problems down the road.

One welcome surprise in our Emily's cancer experience has been the caring response of her peers. People warned us that children would be cruel in their remarks, actions, and teasing. We've had none of that. In fact, her peers have acted more maturely than some adults. We attribute this to a visit from Emily's nurse and to the opportunity to ask questions.

Emily's nurse visited Emily's fourth-grade class when she returned to school following the diagnosis of and initial treatment for leukemia. The nurse explained to classmates, teachers, and the principal exactly what had happened to Emily in the hospital and what would happen in the days ahead. The children asked questions from the simple, "Does the hair fall out like shedding?" to nobody-knows-the-answer questions like, "Why did she get cancer?" The nurse answered honestly and complimented the class on their brilliant questions. She guided them to list ways they could help Emily during the rough days ahead. Emily's cancer fight became a team project, with her classmates participating. In Emily's words, "They forgot all about the cancer and treated me normally." The only hint of cruelty was from a peer in another class who had not heard the presentation. He told Emily it was against the rules to wear a hat to school. Emily's classmates were

> We have discovered ignorance to be the precursor to cruelty. Information and understanding give children the certainty and tools to be genuine friends.

the ones who explained about her balding head and the principal's permission to wear a hat.

Because the children understood what was going on, they responded in caring ways. Some doubted the ability of fourth-graders to understand such complex information. But the children did beautifully. Because they were permitted to ask questions, they were freed to look past the disease to the person on the other side. We have discovered ignorance to be the precursor to cruelty. Information and understanding give children the certainty and tools to be genuine friends.

Bonus Resources

To find books, pamphlets, coloring books, posters, and other literature on your child's crisis, contact societies and associations who address your child's need. Ask about free and for-a-fee resources. To find these groups, check the white pages of your phone book, call the 800 directory (1-800-555-1212), search the Internet, talk to other parents, and ask your medical team or school authorities for names and addresses. Ask also for names of children the same age who face the same challenges. This offers opportunity to build friendships and to discover materials and actions that have helped another child.

MAKE IT FUN

As you teach your child's friends and teachers about his crisis, make the presentation simple and "rememberable." Any kind of printed information, rhyme, or involvement tool can do this. When we summarized the nurse's information for church friends and for use in later grades, we used a five-fact list that spelled a word. We also used a crossword puzzle (see p. 74) that Emily helped compose. What word might spell the facts of your child's crisis? We gave children this C.H.A.S.E. list, overviewed it, and then invited volunteers to name the five facts from memory. The challenge took everyone's mind off being nervous.

Cancer: *Emily has leukemia, which is a kind of cancer.* Cancer means that crazy cells or, more accurately, lazy cells that don't do their job, are growing. Her cancer is in the bone marrow, where blood cells are made. So her cancer affects her blood, making her tired and prone to long fevers.

Have to stop it: *To cure cancer you have to stop the wrong cells and start the right ones again.* The medicines take away the cancer cells' food, keep them from growing, or kill them. Emily takes chemotherapy in pill form every night, and she goes to the hospital every four weeks for shots and checkups. She'll miss school on those days. You may feel jealous about her getting out of school, but she'd choose school over getting shots.

Active no more: *Emily's cancer is now in remission, which means it is no longer active.* But because leukemia cells hide or come back, Emily will keep taking chemotherapy for two years. This part is called maintenance treatment. Doctors have discovered that two years of maintenance produces cure in most cases. That's what we're praying for and working toward.

Side effects: *The chemotherapy medicine she takes has side effects, which means extra things you don't need or want.* These side effects include hurting hips, slow walking, hair loss, and feeling tired. Her hair falls out because chemotherapy goes after fast-growing cells and hair is the fastest-growing cell in our bodies. The chemo thinks hair is a cancer cell. The one good thing about this is that she got curls when her hair grew back in.

Exception to most sicknesses: *Unlike other illnesses, you can't catch leukemia from Emily, so you don't have to worry* *about being around her.* Emily needs you to be her friend and treat her just as if the cancer isn't there. Treat her well, enjoy her fully, and have fun being friends. But if you're sick, stay away from her. Your illnesses can make her ten times more ill. Cancer is also an exception in that it takes a long time to get better.

Love Notes

Offer to help your friend compose a puzzle or presentation for her child's church or school class. Ask her to jot down what she wants said. Write clues from this information and then chart a crossword puzzle on graph paper. You can also create a word search by hiding the answers to the clues in a block of letters.

As a parent of a child in crisis, invite your child to help with the composition of presentations to his classmates. Children like to design crossword puzzles, word searches, and other fun-to-do formats. Including your child in the composition ensures that what the puzzle or activity includes is what your child wants said.

To create a crossword puzzle:

1. List what you want said.

2. Change that list into clues and one-word answers.

3. Chart the answers on graph paper, starting with the longest word.

4. Order and number the clues to match the puzzle.

5. As you present the information, point out answers to the puzzle, pausing while students fill them in.

When Emily entered middle school, she changed from one classroom to six. We spoke to all ninety of her classmates, challenging them to work a printed crossword puzzle as I shared the answers. Emily wrote the answers to the crossword puzzle displayed on an overhead and helped answer questions. We showed the Charlie Brown video on leukemia, pausing it to share tips and ideas.

ACROSS

1. Form in which home chemotherapy comes.
5. The fastest-growing cells in your body. The chemotherapy knows a cancer cell because cancer cells grow fast. Often the chemotherapy gets confused and kills these instead, resulting in thin hair or no hair at all.
6. A simple word for chemotherapy.
7. The place Emily gets most of her shots. The nurses take blood from it and put chemotherapy in it. It is a direct line to the blood system.
9. Where Emily goes for her intensive chemotherapy.
10. The shot that goes into Emily's spine to protect her brain and spinal cord from leukemia cells.
12. What makes Emily feel sad, tired, sleepy, bored, and rotten after the treatments. The worst one is pain in her hips and other joints (TWO WORDS).
13. Where blood is made and where leukemia happens. Also the name of a shot/test.
14. Can you catch leukemia from Emily?
15. Chemotherapy works by taking away the cancer cells' _____ (15 ACROSS), keeps them from _____ing, (4 DOWN) OR _____ (18 ACROSS) them.
17. What is used to cure leukemia (stop the cancer cells from growing and give the healthy cells a chance to start again).

18. Chemotherapy works by taking away the cancer cells' _____ (15 ACROSS), keeps them from _____ing, (4 DOWN) or _____ (18 ACROSS) them.

19. What children used to do from leukemia but usually don't today.

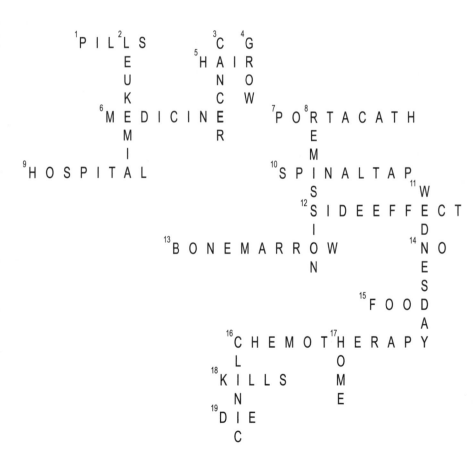

DOWN

2. Name of the cancer Emily is fighting.

3. Means lazy cells that don't do their job are growing rapidly. Emily's kind was in the bone marrow, where blood cells are made. Instead of healthy disease-fighting cells, oxygen-carrying cells, and blood-clotting cells, these kinds of cells were growing. They refuse to fight infection or carry oxygen or clot blood or do anything but multiply. So hers affected her blood, making her tired and prone to fevers.

4. Chemotherapy works by taking away the cancer cells' _____ (15 ACROSS), keeps them from _____ing, (4 DOWN) or _____ (18 ACROSS) them.

8. When leukemia is no longer active.

11. Emily goes to clinic (the hospital) every fourth _____.

16. What we call the hospital for short.

17. Where Emily takes most of her chemotherapy by pill.

INVOLVE THE CHILDREN

For younger children, consider a story approach. Zoe told this story* to her hearing-impaired son's kindergarten classroom, inviting them to respond during the story.

"You like to understand important things, don't you?" asked Zoe.

"Yes!" responded the children enthusiastically.

---

*This story is adapted from *More* January 1993 © Copyright 1992 The Sunday School Board of the Southern Baptist Convention. All rights reserved. Used by permission.

"Good! What do you do when the TV is too quiet?" asked Zoe.

"I turn it up," said Jonathan.

"Well, Seth's ears don't hear loud enough; and he'd like to turn them up. But there's no button on our ears so Seth wears two hearing aids. Seth, will you show them?" said Zoe.

While Seth showed his hearing aids to his friends, Zoe continued, "Seth has worn these hearing aids since he was a baby. No one knows why his ears don't hear louder, but we do know it was nothing he did or didn't do. We are glad for the hearing aids because they make sounds louder. Seth is called 'hard of hearing.' Do you know why?"

"Because hearing is hard for him?" said Sally.

"Exactly," said Zoe. "Seth has to work hard to hear and understand. Hearing aids help, but sometimes he won't understand you, especially when he gets far away from you," said Zoe. "Some people yell when that happens. How do you feel when someone yells at you?"

"Like I'm in trouble," said David.

"I get scared," added Andrea.

"I wonder if someone is mad at me," said Toshio.

"Nobody likes to be yelled at," agreed Zoe. "So when Seth doesn't hear you, move closer, don't get louder. Let's repeat, 'CLOSER not LOUDER.' "

"CLOSER not LOUDER," said the class.

"But sometimes even when I'm close, he doesn't understand me," said Toshio.

"You're right," said Zoe. "In that case, you need to say it a different way. Sounds like *g, k,* and *s* are hard to hear. Sounds like *b* and *d* sound alike. Words with those letters may be hard to understand. Rhyming words can also be confusing. Can you name rhyming words?"

"Sing and ring," said Andrea.

"Bell and yell and fell and well," said Jonathan.

"Right and might and night," said Toshio.

"Ate and hate," added Elise.

"Very good!" said Zoe. "Now let's see what might happen when you use those words in a sentence: 'I hate my sister,' might sound like, 'I *ate* my sister.'" Zoe crossed out "hate" and wrote, "ate" on the chalkboard.

In the midst of laughter, Zoe explained, "Misunderstanding can make things pretty funny. If Seth misunderstands, say the sentence a different way. How might you say it?"

"My sister makes me mad!" said Elise.

"Excellent! What other funny meanings might come from rhyming words?" Zoe invited.

" 'Wait till night,' might sound like, 'wait till light.' " suggested Mei.

"Good! Can you make it clearer?" said Zoe.

"Wait until it turns dark outside?" suggested Mei.

"Excellent! So there are two ways to help Seth understand you. What are they?" asked Zoe.

"Closer not louder," said several students in unison.

"Say it a different way," added Toshio.

"Exactly right," said Zoe. "You can also spell the word, or write it down. Hearing is a big problem for Seth, but it's only one part of his life. He does other things just like you do. What are some things Seth does just like you?"

"Play," said Toshio. "He's good at basketball."

"He does just what our teacher tells him," said Andrea.

"He finishes his work on time and does it neatly," said Mei.

"He smiles and talks," said David.

"Great list," said Zoe. "The only thing he does differently

is hear. So what do you think? Can you and Seth be friends?"

"YES!" shouted the children enthusiastically.

"Have fun being friends to each other!" closed Zoe.

PUT IT ON PAPER

My youth and adult friends frequently hold back from asking me questions about Emily's cancer or Sarah's hearing loss, possibly because they fear upsetting me. Or they don't know how or what to ask, or they don't want to bother me. To help meet their desire to understand, we submit periodic letters for the church newsletter and write longer tip sheets for Sunday School teachers and others who work directly with our children. We also submit resources to our church and school libraries. We give coloring books on the crises to our daughter's friends, cousins, and classmates. Every time we find something that helps us understand, we try to share it with others.

Our newsletter entries look something like this:

Dear Church Family,

We are pleased to share that Emily is still in remission from acute lymphocytic leukemia. We continue with maintenance treatments that consist of daily chemotherapy in pill form and more intensive chemotherapy at the hospital every four weeks. This fourth week is rough physically and emotionally because the chemotherapy is so intense. Thus we currently have one very painful week during which the chemotherapy builds up in her system, and three weeks during which Emily feels good and feels like herself. Our next three hospital visits are July 24, August 21, and September 18. Please hold us up in prayer on those days and the seven days afterward when the side effects are so difficult.

Please pray also for her remission (absence of active disease) to last forever and for protection of Emily through chemotherapy.

The uncertainty and pain are very difficulty, but we have great hope and are glad we have medicine and doctors to help us in our fight against cancer. Second Corinthians 4:8, Lamentations 3:22-23, and Deuteronomy 33:27 have been so true for us.

Thank you for listening, loving, and meeting our needs.

The Dockreys

We offer this tip sheet to Emily's school and church teachers:

Dear Teachers:

Emily is undergoing maintenance chemotherapy to prevent the return of leukemia. She was diagnosed in November of last year and has been in remission (absence of active disease) since December. She takes combination chemotherapy, including pills every day at home and then an intense "pulse" of medicine every four weeks. We call this pulse treatment "chemo week." Her continuing side effect from chemotherapy is weakness in her legs that makes it hard to run or to climb stairs. She likes sports, so go ahead and encourage her to do everything. Activity is not physically dangerous—in fact, exercise can compensate for her leg weakness (due to neurotoxicity of the medicine).

Emily's chemo week comes every fourth week. She has three good weeks when she feels like herself. Then during this fourth week she receives the intensive drugs that give her the most troublesome side effects. During this week the chemicals that attack any returning cancer also attack her.

Emily's chemo week usually goes like this:

Tuesday

Anticipates the pain of needles. Sometimes she forgets it's coming and then she doesn't worry.

Wednesday

Goes to the hospital for checkup and chemotherapy. Most visits include drawing blood and receiving IV chemo. Every third visit is a spinal tap to protect the brain and central nervous system.

Thursday/Friday

Feels tired but usually few "feelable" side effects. Back will hurt some after spinal tap. Usually few complaints at home, none at school.

Saturday/Sunday/Monday

The worst side effect days. Emily's joints hurt, her stomach hurts (not nausea but a burning feeling), she's physically tired from lack of sleep (caused by the medicine), and she's sad (caused by the medicine).

Tuesday/Wednesday

Returning to normal. Feels like self again by about Tuesday evening. May lose a little hair this week but seldom noticeable.

The best antidote to the side effects is intriguing activity. We can't stop the pain, so we have to take her mind off it. Thanks for loving her. She seldom complains, and we appreciate her good attitude.

We approach the cancer treatment matter-of-factly, assuming that informed peers are caring peers. I'm attaching a crossword puzzle* we have used in the past. If you like, I will come and explain the cancer-fighting process and tell how it affects Emily, using the crossword puzzle as a guide. We also have the thirty-minute Charlie Brown video on leukemia, which is excellent and accurate—we'd be glad for you to show it sometime. Please feel free to call with questions or concerns.

The Dockreys

P.S. Emily is comfortable talking about her leukemia. Please feel free to ask her or us questions at any time. It won't hurt our feelings—in fact, it makes us feel more loved.

---

* In this book on pages 74-75.

KEEP TALKING

"The first person who told me about Sarah said she was deaf," shared a friend, pleasantly surprised with how easy she found it to talk with Sarah. "Because of that I never had spoken to her."

Even with our best efforts, someone misunderstood the nature of Sarah's hearing loss. With hearing aids she hears almost as well as her hearing peers, she needs no sign language, and she's definitely not dumb. We've learned to keep on listening, answering questions, and sharing information. The process can be emotionally exhausting and painful, but we must do it for the sake of our children.

Love Notes

Be the friend who spreads accurate information about a child's crisis. Ask the parents what they want people to know about their child and how they want people to treat her. Then spread those words. Refuse to improvise.

TWELVE WAYS TO HELP

Families of children in crisis suggest these twelve practical ways to help. Remember to choose the action that helps the family, rather than the one you like best. For example, your friend may have a freezer full of food but need someone to bring homework from school daily.

1. Find out the child's favorite foods and bring those. The casserole you love may not please a child.

2. Substitute for the church class your friend teaches. Caring for this church family frees your friend to care for his at-home family.

3. Do one or more of the family's daily chores, such as grocery shopping, laundry, errand running. Pick up and return laundry. Call when you're going, or run errands specifically for your friend.

4. Bring food in disposable containers and offer to return nondisposable containers brought by others.

5. Find out the child's favorite games and play them with him.

6. Shop for a hard-to-find item, such as comfortable clothes to fit a wheelchair-bound child, or a cute hat to cover a chemotherapy-induced bald head.

7. Bring a series of open-one-a-day presents to help a child through the chicken pox, a hospitalization, or another long ordeal. Wrap each gift and number it. This gives a child (and parent) something to look forward to daily. Even if the "child" is 25, this is still a fun care-giving strategy.

8. Send "This is what you mean to me and why" letters to the parents. When overwhelmed with their child's crisis, they need the encouragement of knowing their lives make a difference. You don't have to say anything about the crisis.

9. Serve as information coordinator. Be the one to repeat the symptoms, next step, specific needs, current prayer requests, and praises. Ask your friend what to communicate rather than decide yourself what to say.

10. Ask for specific prayer needs. Then pray for these.

11. Give attention to siblings who feel left out when their sick or injured sibling gets most of the attention. Write letters, send sticker books, spend special time together, bring tiny gifts, and more.

12. Listen. Don't try to explain, interpret, "blessing-ize," or diagnose. Simply hear your friend's story and feel along. It's nearly impossible to find someone who will hear the details.

THE POINT ←——

As you and your child walk through crises, notice and cherish the loving friends God sends your way. Receive their spontaneous acts of love, and work with them to find other ways to care for you and your child.

"JUST LET ME KNOW IF THERE'S ANYTHING I CAN DO"

I've discovered that more people care than show it. When people say, "Let me know if there's anything I can do," I'm learning to answer with something specific. I offer two or three specific actions, one very simple and one more complex. Then friends can choose the one they most want to do. I've also learned to keep a list, because what I need doesn't always come readily to mind.

Friends feel better if they can do something. You're not being greedy when you let friends care; you're freeing them to love your child in a way he needs loving. You're equipping them to do the something they want to do. If you feel uneasy answering the "what can I do?" question directly, write a list of your needs and give it to a trusted friend who can answer the question for you.

FOCUS ON FRIENDS WHO CARE

Some people will torment you with their plastic phrases of promised well-being. Some friends and family members will withdraw from you because they are unwilling to suffer with you. Limit your contact with these comforters of Job who don't mean to hurt you, but do.

Then turn to those treasured friends who genuinely care. These "for better/for worse" friends don't mind asking you how you really are. They listen whether the news is painful or joyous. They don't worry about your tears or your fears. They refuse to run from your pain. They strengthen you to face the challenges ahead simply by loving you.

Chapter 5

Walk On Through Anger

"Do not let your anger lead you into sin."
Ephesians 4:26 (GNB)

I was unprepared for the deep rage which grew in me as the reality of my daughter's cystic fibrosis sank in," explained Elsa. "I expected sadness but not anger. Each day that passed showed me more uncertainty coupled with never-ending infections. I looked for someone to blame. Oddly enough, the person I blamed was my cousin. She had nothing to do with my daughter's illness, so my anger was illogical. But it persisted just the same. I guess it began when she calmly informed me that my daughter's illness would spiritually purify me. Her easy answers angered rather than comforted me. I wanted her to receive some of the 'blessings' she was so certain I would enjoy.

"My anger deepened as she complained about little things—she went on and on about her broken toaster as though it was the end of the world. I had to bite my tongue to keep from saying, 'Will you look at what you have? Three healthy sons who seldom get so much as a twenty-four-hour virus, time free of doctor visits and hospital stays, the promise of long life. How can you complain when you have so much?' I became defensive when she fussed about the way her children behaved but did nothing to teach them how to mind. Here I was trying to help my chronically ill daughter be kind and thoughtful, and my cousin did little to develop the character of her healthy sons. I wanted to shout, 'Why don't you appreciate life?'

"I found myself similarly enraged when I'd hear a mother scream at her child in the grocery store. My daughter faced progressive illness that would likely steal her young life, and this mother slandered her healthy daughter. Still another mother with a precious two-year-old complained that she was too old to be chasing a toddler. I cherished my daughter, and this mother wanted to be rid of hers. Why couldn't these mothers value their children? Why couldn't they share some of the pain?

"I kept telling myself I was having a pity party. I reminded myself that pain is pain and their worries seem as deep to them as my worries are to me. At the same time, a child fighting for breath seems a little more important than a broken toaster. As I reminded myself that my attitude is the only one I can change and that my daughter and I share moments of great joy, I felt guilty for my anger. My mind calmed down, but my anger raged on. No |matter how I tried to talk myself out of these feelings, they persisted. I'm finally discovering that I've got to go ahead and feel the anger when it comes."

SEE ANGER AS A SIGN OF PAIN

Elsa is right. Anger is a sign of pain. She can no more stop the anger than she can wish away her daughter's cystic fibrosis. Once she walks through the anger, the rage will ease and she'll discover what action, if any, she needs to take. Elsa has discovered that the only path around anger is through it. Elsa also recognizes that anger is the emotion most Christians have the hardest time expressing.

Elsa can ignore her anger, but it won't go away. Anger always finds a way out. Unaddressed anger will hurt Elsa through depression, hurt her family through her irritability, or hurt her cousin through sarcasm. Suppressed anger comes out as cold treatment, criticism, unprovoked attacks, vengefulness, or worse.

> The only path around anger is through it.

Elsa can let her anger out unharnessed, but it would become a cruel attack, a bitter accusation, a shouting match, a feud, or a lasting alienation.

Instead of either of these, Elsa chooses to let her anger become a healer. She follows the Ephesians 4:26 prescription: "Be ye angry and sin not" (KJV).

To be angry, Elsa doesn't have to attack her cousin, the stranger in the supermarket, or the friend with the toddler. She doesn't even have to voice her anger out loud. But she must take action. She must walk on through her fury in a redemptive way. As she feels her anger, talks to God about it, thinks it through, and decides what to do next, her anger dissolves.

Sometimes Elsa walks through her anger privately by way of praying, journaling, or remembering. Other times she talks it out with her husband or a friend. Still other times she mentally composes a conversation with her cousin or writes her cousin a letter telling her just how she feels. Elsa edits out destructive words and attitudes and then decides, together with God, whether to talk with her cousin or not. She always destroys the letter knowing that face-to-face communication is better for this type of conflict.

Many times just thinking through the anger or composing an internal conversation is enough. Other times God directs Elsa to share her thoughts with someone who angers her in hopes that the accidental, but still painful, hurting will stop. Elsa listens for God's direction and lets Him heal her through the actions He specifies.

ACCEPT YOUR CHILD'S ANGER

Ten-year-old Kirk threw his pencil across the room. "I hate that tumor. It makes it impossible to concentrate!" When he was seven, an optic nerve tumor stole all sight from Kirk's left eye and half the sight from his right. The tumor, combined with aftereffects of tumor-halting radiation, has doubled the time Kirk must spend completing school assignments. Most days he works with diligence and discipline. Some days it just gets to him.

Kirk's outburst shocked his dad. He scolded, "Control yourself, Kirk!" Startled by his own shouting, Dad added, "I must admit, at least you've got your anger directed at the right place. I don't like that tumor either."

Kirk is right to be angry. Neither the tumor nor its consequences are good. They are distortions of God's good creation. The tumor and radiation side effects have created tremendous problems. God is sad about these problems along with us. There's nothing good about them. They can't glorify God. But the way Kirk responds to them can.

Kirk's anger becomes wrong only when Kirk does destructive things with it (recall Eph. 4:26). He must not break lamps or torment his sister. He must find a positive path through the pain. Kirk's learning problems are real. But even more real is the power God offers to manage those problems. Kirk can glorify God by the way he responds to sad circumstances. Kirk and his parents can refuse to let evil steal their joy. They can let God poke His joy into the bad situations. They can express their anger positively. They can depend on God for strength and trust Him for security. These are the actions that demonstrate God's power. These are the moves that glorify God.

> Anger is a rough section on every road of pain. We can't detour around it; we've got to go on through it.

These moves do not happen instantly—glorifying God is a journey. As on most journeys, there are smooth and bumpy sections of road. Anger is a rough section on every road of pain. We can't detour around it; we've got to go on through it.

Only by walking on through anger can we and our children find the "peace that passeth understanding" (Phil. 4:7 KJV).

GUIDE YOUR CHILD THROUGH ANGER

Though children freely express their anger, they can't always walk through it as calmly as adults can (and we're not always models of composure). Nor can they recognize the healing power of anger. They simply feel mad, and that scares them. To calm your child's fear, first notice the strengths in your child's anger. Kirk's anger has two strengths:

(1) *It's honest and direct.* Both Kirk and his dad know how he feels and why. Kirk's direct and honest anger can heal both him and his dad. Throwing the pencil may not be the best expression of anger, but it is better than flipping over the table. Once Kirk has opened his anger, he can pour out the rest more gently.

(2) *It's directed toward the right source.* Rather than blame God, the doctors, or his schoolteacher, Kirk directs his anger at the cause of his misery—the tumor. The tumor is an exploitation of God's perfect creation. It is perfectly appropriate to get mad at such insults to God. The tumor does not glorify God. The tumor attacks the good that God creates.

Continue to ease your child's agitation by inviting him to tell you more about why he's mad. You may first have to help him burn off the intensity of the anger so he can talk or think or act on the anger. Try:

A hug. Hold your child and let the angry tears come. Human touch communicates the stability and love that children need to express their anger and to thrive under even the toughest of conditions.

Anger-absorbing toys. When two-year-old Patricia enters tantrum mode, her dad points out her bop bag. The sturdy plastic clown bounces back no matter how much Patricia jumps on it, punches it, or pounds it. Once the bop bag has absorbed Patricia's physical anger, she can talk out her feelings. Her older brother uses a punching bag.

Personal sports. Don't send your child into competitive play angry, but let him privately eat up anger by shooting baskets, working with weights, or jogging. Suggest your child name the hoop, ball, weight, or distance with the cause of his anger, and then attack it.

Physical activity. Work can also absorb anger. As your child attacks each log he chops or each bit of dust he vacuums, the physical activity consumes the energy of the anger, and the mind prays through the reason.

A private spot. Some children calm down only with time alone. Give these children a private place to harness their anger before they try to drive it home. If your child's anger accelerates rather than calms when you talk with him, encourage him to take time in his room or another thinking spot to get it together. Once he spends time in his room thinking, crying, or stomping, he emerges cleansed and humbled, ready to work things through.

A poem, letter, or song. Offer your child ideas for expressing anger with vigor. When your high-schooler is angry about a friend's injury, suggest he write a poem about what the friend means to him. When your middle-schooler is upset with a teacher, guide her to pen a letter including exactly what she feels like doing to him. Then remind her to tear up the letter (an anger-reducer itself) and throw away the rage. When your first-grader is mad at the rain that postponed the picnic, compose a song about rain.

Prayer. While your child hits the punching bag, burns energy with sports, thinks privately, or writes out anger, suggest she invite God along. God will heal anger through listening, understanding, and loving. Many children and adults hesitate to tell God about their anger, fearing He doesn't like it. But God created anger; it accomplishes good purposes when used in His ways.

Turn the anger into action and the action into healing.

When your child is ready to talk, offer to be his comrade. Listen as he tells you about his anger. Invite his thoughts with questions like: "What happened?" "Why does it make you so mad?" "What do you wish you could change?" "Which parts can't be changed no matter how much you want them to change?" "What do you think we should do?" "How can God help us?"

Just letting anger out calms it, soothes your child, and enables both of you to act on it. Listen more than you talk; hug more than you prescribe. If your child refuses to talk, insist that he say at least three sentences. This testing time will show him that his feelings make sense, that you will understand, and that together you can find solutions.

Once your child has reduced the intense anger and talked with you about it, the two of you can discover what to do next. Sometimes just expressing the anger is enough. Other times your child needs more. You and your disappointed-about-the-rained-out-picnic first-grader may want to hold an indoor picnic. You and your middle-schooler might do something away from school to demonstrate that the troublesome teacher is not the only factor in her life. You and your high-schooler may need to visit his hospitalized friend and find ways to keep in touch.

Neither you nor your child can get to the healing unless you go through the anger. Equally important, you won't find the healing if you stop in the middle of the anger. Go on through and keep going until you're both on the other side.

Child's Viewpoint

Anger scares children. The emotion can be so intense that they feel out of control, which intensifies both their fear and their anger. Children of all ages need the stability a parent can give through hugs, helps, assurance that they'll handle it together, and affirmation that the feeling makes sense. Be close both physically and emotionally as you guide your child through anger to the solution on the other side.

DIRECT YOUR ANGER AT THE SOURCE

Many people turn their anger toward God, but He's the healer of anger, not the cause of it. If you find yourself angry at God, tell Him about it. As you talk, He'll love and heal you. Then He'll help you turn your anger toward the real cause.

A person, place, thing, or circumstance can spark anger in you or your child. Anger generators include:

• circumstances like birth defects or misuse of power;

• people who act cruelly or say thoughtless things;

• places that remind you of an injustice or injury;

• things such as germs and guns and alcohol.

"Why does everything happen to me?" nine-year-old Ericka lamented. "Amanda never misses Christmas. Somebody in our family always gets sick on holidays. It's not fair!"

Ericka's anger was generated by a cousin's germ. The illness kept her extended family from getting together. Ericka is yelling about Amanda, but Amanda is not the problem. Her dad helps her isolate the anger generator with: "That dumb germ! I wish it hadn't come to our house!"

"Yeah," said Ericka. "I wish it would go to the devil!"

They recognized the anger, felt it, figured out what to do about it, and moved on.

By pinpointing the cause for the problem, Ericka and her dad have given the anger a place to land. Ericka can "be angry and sin not" (Eph. 4:26) by directing her anger at the germ rather than her friend. She can yell at the germ instead of tormenting her brother.

"Let's tell it not to stay around long," suggested Ericka's dad. "And in the meantime we won't let this germ-that-stole-Christmas steal our joy. We'll just have our own little celebration here. We've already had our family Christmas, but we've wanted to watch that movie series. Why don't we rent it and have a movie marathon?"

"Yeah!" cried Ericka and her brother.

"But when will we get to have Christmas with Grandma and Grandpa?" recalled Ericka.

"Whenever everyone gets better. The presents will wait, and we'll leave the tree up as long as we need to," said Ericka's dad.

"Good," said Ericka. "I wish we could go today."

"Me, too," echoed Ericka's brother, mom, and dad.

The family took a few minutes just to sit together and be sad. Then they piled into the car and traveled to the video rental store singing about the germ that stole Christmas (a distant cousin of the Grinch). Nobody liked the fact that they had to miss their Christmas gathering, but feeling the disappointment together helped them all heal. They recognized the anger, felt it, figured out what to do about it, and moved on.

It was OK for Ericka to be angry. It was OK for her to say so. It would not have been OK for her to slam doors, throw plates, grump at her family, or stay mad. As her parents listened to Ericka's anger and agreed that it made them mad too, Ericka felt more like discovering a solution to the anger. As the family lamented together and attacked the source of the anger, their companionship made the problem less lonesome.

Words like "you'll get over it" and "don't get all upset" would have done little to comfort Ericka. If Ericka's parents had refused to let her be disappointed and angry, Ericka would have felt not only angry but also guilty for feeling angry. Her parents would have abandoned her to suffer alone and more acutely. She'd have had little interest in a solution. She'd have remained cross and grouchy. Walking through the anger with Ericka kept her anger shorter and safer.

RECOGNIZE THAT PAIN
IS NOT THE OPPOSITE OF FAITH

Sadly, fellow Christians can generate some of the strongest anger in us. Maybe it's because we expect more compassion from them. Maybe it's because they feel we should walk right through problems without a hitch. Maybe it's because they don't think Christians should be sad.

"I'm amazed at how badly the church handles long-term crises," claims Andrew. "They do great that first week or two, bringing meals and gifts for the children. But then everybody wants us to get all better. They want us to say we're fine. They want to push away our sadness. My pastor even told me to go on antidepressants so my grief wouldn't last as long."

"There are so many people in my church who have avoided me since my daughter's death," says Barbara. "I think it's because I represent a painful reality—the suffering and death of a child. Children aren't supposed to get sick and die. People don't know what to say or do, so they just stay away. The time I need them the most, they abandon me.

"Many of my fellow Christians just won't face it. They ignore me, make me a hero, or quote Bible phrases like 'all things work together for good.' Quoting things may make everything OK for them, but it makes me angry. Their quotes come across as faith challenges that say, 'If you were a good Christian, you'd know this Bible verse and you wouldn't be hurting.' What happened to verses like 'weep with those who weep' (Rom. 12:15)? People are afraid to share my pain.

"In my anger I'm so afraid I'll say something harsh to one of them. I know they mean well, but they hurt me so deeply. Why won't they hug me? Why won't they listen? Why do they keep trying to make everything OK? Why do they pretend that nothing sad has happened? I just wish somebody would care."

Where does this belief that Christians should not hurt come from? Why do so many in the Christian community feel that pain is contrary to faith? The Psalms are full of pain.

> To take heart means to keep your eyes on Jesus, not to dance through the sadness.

Lamentations details the suffering of the Israelites. Hosea's agony over his wife's unfaithfulness went on for years, and God compared His love to Hosea's. The deeply spiritual Paul fought a physical ailment that tormented him and made him weak (2 Cor. 12:7-10).

The Bible records no one hurrying Paul's recovery or criticizing his weakness. Paul identified Satan as the giver of the ailment and credited God for getting him through it. The end result was strength in weakness, but the walk through was a tough one.

Many Christians like the end better than the journey. They have trouble with trouble. But trouble is a part of every life. As Jesus explains, "In this world you will have trouble. But take heart! I have overcome the world" (John 16:33). To take heart means to keep your eyes on Jesus, not to dance through the sadness. To take heart means to demonstrate confidence that we will one day overcome, not that everything is instantly OK.

Barbara knows that she'll see her daughter again in heaven, that her hope in Christ is certain, that God's power will get her through. But the pain and anger are now. God is the author of these emotions. Barbara needs caring Christian people who will walk with her.

Sheila had the opposite, but equally destructive, experience. After her son's sudden death, Christian friends were so complimentary of her smile that Sheila kept right on smiling. She held her pain and anger inside, even convincing herself that she was fine. She pushed aside her deep struggle with the death of her son. As a result, Sheila never fully healed. She still smiles, but now she struggles inwardly with a lack of focus and place. Her surviving daughter is most assuredly spoiled. Apparently Sheila indulged her daughter as a way to love her lost son.

Had Sheila been allowed to grieve, both she and her daughter would be more contented and happy. Instead, Sheila's daughter is angry and lonely. She bears the anger Sheila never resolved. Failing to walk through the sad anger kept Sheila from being an effective parent.

We've got to walk through the darkness to get to the light. There's no way to skip around it. Recall the word "through" in Psalm 23:4, "Yea, though I walk through the valley of the shadow of death, I will fear no evil: for Thou art with me; Thy rod and Thy staff they comfort me" (KJV). Andrew, Barbara, and Sheila need Christian friends to walk with them through the valley of the shadow of death, both for themselves and for their children.

Love Notes

Few Christians accept the reality of pain in this world. They try to explain it away; they make heroes out of those who suffer. Or they pretend it's not really suffering at all but an opportunity to be joyful. Let's break this destructive pattern. Let's recognize painful events for what they are: distortions of God's good plan. Rather than be the cause of a Christian's anger, become a source of compassion. Hear the pain, feel along with your friends, and give them the love they need to make it through the journey unscarred.

To be the valuable friend a parent in crisis is looking for:

Rather than say	**Let's say**
I admire you.	I'm so sorry.
She'll get better; I just know it.	What have the doctors said about her prognosis? What does she have to go through?
Have faith!	I'm glad God is walking through this with you. I'll come along too if you want me.
This will bring you a blessing.	It's hard, isn't it?

Love Notes

Rather than say	**Let's say**
All things work together for good.	I'm sure God is as sad about this as we are.
This happened to you because you're so strong (which comes across as, *"I'm glad it's you and not me"*).	I'm sad this has happened. This world is a dangerous place. What specific things can I do to help?
Don't be angry!	Tell me what makes you maddest.
It could be worse.	This is terrible. Tell me what hurts the most.
You son will make it.	It's a long, hard road, isn't it?

As we hear anger from friends, they feel the love of Christ through us. They are empowered rather than abandoned. They have more energy for parenting both the child in crisis and their other children.

STOP THE SIN

Hannah remembers her mother's continual anger at her father. Every time something went wrong, she blamed him. She blamed him for weather, community events, and other things that could in no way be his fault. As a child, Hannah hated having to choose sides. She vowed never to let her anger do that to her family. But when her son is feeling bad and Hannah becomes especially tired, the old family pattern creeps into Hannah's life. She greets her husband with, "You told me you'd be home at 5:30. It's 6:00, and the pork chops are burned! What do you mean you want to watch the news special? We've been holding supper for you. The least you can do is eat with us!"

Hannah never recognizes what's happening until it's too late, until her fussing and picking have set the stage for a tense dinner and uncommunicative evening. Her mother's anger pattern has traveled through time to torment Hannah, her husband, and their children.

Hannah experiences firsthand Deuteronomy 5:9—the sins of her parents have visited the third generation. Hannah is just plain mad about this. But rather than stop there, as her mother did, Hannah lets her regret and her anger motivate her to stop the anger pattern and the controlling tendencies, to start a caring pattern that will travel down the generations. No matter how hard her current crisis becomes, she decides to live Deuteronomy 5:10, the blessing pattern, instead.

It takes work, deliberately halting caustic words before they exit her mouth. It takes intentional compassion, seeing her husband's needs and her children's point of view. It takes refusal to abuse anger, and it takes commitment to turn anger into care. All this work is multiplied when crises come and nerves are raw. But Hannah must do it, for the sake of her family, for her own sake, for God's sake.

Anger is a powerful force, determined to express itself in some way, prone toward destruction. Hannah recognizes anger's power, having seen what happens when anger flails unharnessed. She determines to use anger as a motivation for good, for building up. With God's help, she'll stop the sin that is controlling her.

In the process of halting sin, Hannah must take the same path through anger that Elsa and Kirk have taken. She lets the feelings come, turning her focus toward the One who can help her sort them out: "God, what can I do to control my rage? How can I leave the past and move on? Teach me to transform my anger into healing."

> Anger is a powerful force, determined to express itself in some way, prone toward destruction.

On and on she prays, until the anger eases away. Sometimes it takes minutes, sometimes hours, sometimes days. Like most anger, Hannah's rage stems from pain—pain that she has hurt her family, pain that her mother has hurt her. Hannah's anger provides both cleansing and opportunity. She finds cleansing through feeling the anger. She finds opportunity through focusing on ways to care for her husband and children next time. She walks through anger until there's no more of it to walk through. She determines to stop the sin before it grows again.

LET ANGER GO

Once you've walked through anger, let it go. Refuse to abuse anger by enjoying it, by dwelling on it, by wallowing in it. Hannah's mother has stayed mad at her husband for over thirty years. Her health, her marriage, her children, and her grandchildren suffer as a result. Walk on through the anger. Then leave it behind, where it belongs.

This won't be easy. An encounter with anger is seldom over in one instance. Elsa may get mad every time she hears a parent complain about a healthy child. Kirk will again become angry with the tumor that has tormented him for over six years. Andrew and Barbara will feel that all-too-familiar rage when church friends say well-meaning but thoughtless things. But each encounter can grow milder until the anger dissipates.

We'll never be totally past anger this side of heaven, but we don't have to do reruns. Eventually, we can keep from repeating the same anger about the same circumstance. Each time anger comes, recognize it, feel it, think and pray through it, figure out what to do about it, and move on. Move through anger assured that you can't move past it except by going through it. Don't expect logical and clean solutions. But expect certain solutions.

Deal with your anger instance by instance, remembering that anger is not bad in and of itself, but is a good gift from a good God for a good purpose. Anger is powerful and very dangerous if used wrongly, but we need not fear anger in ourselves or fellow Christians. Anger grows when it's neglected, not when it's addressed. We can walk through it to keep it from growing wild. We can pray through it to disable it once and for all.

THE POINT ⟵

Both parents and children feel angry in crises. This anger seeks a place to land. Allow yourself and your child to feel this anger fully, to point it toward the target that caused the pain, and to take action to resolve the anger. Walk through anger confidently, assured that, unless you do, you cannot live your faith effectively.

Chapter 6

Let Your Child Be a Child

"At the moment they stop being a kid and turn into a child with cancer, the smiles disappear. Every face around them reflects a mixture of sadness, shock, pity, or—worse—reverence for someone chosen to suffer."
—Erma Bombeck

I grew up with double scoliosis, a progressive curvature of my spine. In the eighth grade I had twenty-three vertebrae fused together to straighten my back," explains Trish. "After the surgery I was fitted with a torso cast to wear for nine months. I could move from place to place, but I found it hard to sit and found only a few clothes that fit. I figured I could do anything for nine months. Then those nine months stretched into four long years—the donor bone used in the grafts was infected. I had numerous surgeries to clean out the staph infection that spread throughout my back, and I was recasted several times. Each time they promised they'd take the cast off the next visit. Each time I prayed they'd be right. Time after time I was disappointed.

"The interesting thing looking back is that I don't remember being sick. I missed about six weeks of school following my initial surgery, but before and after that I went to school every day. I did not grieve for 'normalcy' because I had never been through childhood or adolescence any other way. Instead I was excited about each new year. I attacked my challenges with vigor and anticipation. The only thing I backed away from was boys. I couldn't imagine going on a date in my cast, so I avoided boys.

"I don't remember feeling sorry for myself except for maybe an hour or so. I knew my parents felt bad that their poor daughter had to go through all this, but they didn't let me hide behind my problems. They would never let me stay home with the grumps or the cramps. Their confidence in me, plus my own determination to stay involved with life, led to such adventures as marching with the band in 118-degree weather. We had to remake a band uniform to fit over my body cast and then cool me off between marches by blowing out the cast with a vacuum on reverse.

"It's not that I felt strong or especially gifted, I just didn't want to miss anything. Life was to be lived and I knew it. As a result, though I stayed in the hospital frequently and went through incredible pain, I don't feel like I missed out."

What's the secret? How did Trish come through such an ordeal unscathed? Three actions stand out.

- Trish's parents let Trish be Trish;

- Trish's parents preserved her childhood; and

- Trish's parents worked as God's ambassadors.

Trish's parents refused to label Trish as "the girl with the body cast." They worked around the body cast to love her as she was. They let Trish dive headfirst into the activities that mattered to her—she marched in the band even when it meant itchy sweat inside a sweltering cast. At the same time they refused to force her into experiences she was not yet ready for—like dating. Rather than pity, they offered compassion. Rather than mask her pain with platitudes like, "You're so brave," they let her be a normal kid. Rather than accept excuses, they equipped her to face her challenges.

"My parents could have worked against my determination by saying stuff like, 'Are you sure you want to?' or, 'You'll get too sweaty in that hot weather.' But they didn't," Trish continued. "If I said I wanted to try something, they found a way to help me do it.

"I think my Christianity had the most to do with how I managed. I spent a lot of time in my room doing homework or Bible study or just thinking. I'd write in my diary, 'Lord, please let me get the cast off during this next checkup. I was supposed to last time and didn't. Let this be the time.' Then I'd go to the doctor and receive the news that my cast would stay on another six months. How does a kid handle that? This happened five times, and the last time I wrote, 'OK, Lord, I don't care. Leave me in this forever. Whatever You want, I'll do. I've been through this cast and I can handle it.' I feel like God used that rough time to show me how to rely on Him.

"I also remember saying to myself that I wouldn't make friends because of good looks and clothes like most kids, that I would have to learn to be outgoing. I made an effort to be friendly to people and it paid off.

"The weird thing is, I think it was harder on my sister than me. She'd get angry or irritated with me and then feel guilty for it. I don't think my parents handled that too well. Because there was no air conditioning, I would position my cast where air would pass through it to cool me off. But that would stink terribly, like B.O.—the inside of the cast was changed only every six months. My sister would say, 'Mom, it stinks! Make her quit!' Instead of encouraging us to work together, Mom would say, 'Cut it out! Poor Trish has to wear that cast. The least you can do is put up with a little smell.' My sister would then feel terrible and I'd gloat."

Trish's parents didn't do everything right. They made mistakes like any parents. But they succeeded grandly at one important thing—they refused to deny Trish her childhood. Big health problems don't make children instant adults, nor should they. Trish attended school, enjoyed the band, opted for adventure, tormented her sister, and participated in routine family life.

Our first reaction as parents of a child in crisis is to cuddle our hurting child close and keep her at home. We must move past protectiveness to solid parenting. We must allow and encourage steady participation in school, church, play, and family life to give our children the rich lives they yearn for. Children in crisis aren't all that different from other children. They long to be treated normally and cherished as the unique people they are.

Love Notes

Express appreciation to the doctors, nurses, teachers, and friends who cherish your child and bring out your child's strengths, confidence, capabilities. Thank them for specific actions you appreciate like:

- "Thanks for helping Jamie take his shots with such strategy. When you tell him he relaxes better than someone twice his age, he feels so capable and pleased."

- "I so appreciate your Bible teaching on Sunday morning and your care that goes beyond Sundays. When you discovered how dangerous it would be for Jenny to get sick, you telephoned every student's family to explain that you had a student with cancer, to explain the situation, and to ask them to let you know if their child had a cold or signs of illness. Then you could warn us so we could stay home that week. Thanks so much."

- "I want to tell you how much I appreciate your staying in pediatric oncology and excelling in it. We parents don't have a choice about going through cancer, but you do. Your choosing to stay means you will hurt when our kids hurt, but it also means our children will survive. Your high level of expertise and competence means our kids will make it. I'm so glad you're walking with us.

CHERISH YOUR CHILD AS A PERSON

Like Trish, your child in crisis is a person. Respect him as a one-of-a-kind precious person, not an extension of you or an imposition on you. Remember this need to be cherished, to be treated with value. Then recognize that he is a child, not a fully matured adult. It is your responsibility to guide him toward maturity, not expect him to make it on his own. Step by step, help him become the loving and competent adult God has in mind.

Notice the unique gifts God has given your child and then work alongside God to water and feed those gifts as they blossom. Don't hesitate to weed out the bad, but do so in ways that don't harm the tender growing gifts. Thank God for the privilege of parenting your child and then take the privilege seriously with intentional action.

Olivia noticed the drastic differences in her two boys. Marc is sensitive, responsive, and consistently obedient. He seems to know what Olivia wants, almost before she asks. His natural helpfulness and expressed kindness make him a delight to be around. He never lacks for something to do—his expansive imagination and endless ideas keep his days full and happy. He's always creating some game or scenario—from animal hospital to survival in the desert. His insights into people and problems lead to loving and effective problem-solving. He has a deep-seated confidence that can't be shaken. Interestingly, he's painfully shy. He balks at meeting new people or trying new experiences.

Julio, on the other hand, is headstrong and determined. He obeys only when Olivia watches. He questions every request with "Do I have to?" or "Does Marc have to do it too?" He becomes easily bored and constantly asks, "What can I do?" But Julio is intensely happy. He sings all the time and will try anything. His imagination runs in a different track than Marc's but is equally persistent. He meets new people with eagerness. He finds friends wherever he goes, both those he's met before and those totally new to him. His smile and adventuresome spirit are delightfully contagious.

For years these differences frustrated Olivia. She considered Marc the easier personality. Yet Marc's struggle with new situations was anything but easy. Julio's relative ease in meeting people jolted Olivia to see her sons in a new light. Julio's confidence in crowds is a direct result of his bold personality. She began to call him passionate rather than stubborn. Julio's deep-feeling nature comes out negatively as rebellion, but quite positively as assertive friendliness. Marc's positive sensitivity makes him entirely comfortable with the familiar, but hesitant to try the new.

Both sons have up and down sides to their personality characteristics. Olivia works to keep the down sides from dominating—she refuses to accept Julio's angry outbursts because they keep Julio from being the caring Christian he wants to be. She refuses to let Marc avoid new situations because he'll miss the discovery that new adventures really are worth trying. Appreciating the up side of down means we focus on the good as we guide our children to eradicate the bad.

Each child can and must learn from the tempering and guiding efforts of his parents. Marc can push himself to say "hello" even when it terrifies him. Julio can replace rebellion with respect. Each son will grow happier and better equipped to manage life as he grows the good and weeds out the bad. Each will find motivation to do this as the good is noticed, rather than the bad resented.

Crises intensify both Marc's and Julio's personality characteristics. Marc reads a book and avoids people when he's feeling sick. Julio stomps and rages in response to infection. Both want extra cuddling. Olivia gives both boys affection in the ways they like best. She then encourages Marc to put down his book long enough to eat and encourages Julio to be kind even when he feels rotten. Appreciation for the strength in both boys gives her the foundation to care specifically.

Children in pain need steady love, high expectations, consistent discipline, stimulating challenge, and loving guidance from the caring adults in their lives. The crisis changes none of these needs, just makes them more complex to meet. No matter how complicated your child's needs become, be the consistent and cherishing adult your child needs. Chapter 3 offers more ideas.

How are your children uniquely wonderful? How do their personality characteristics contribute to the way they handle crises or to the way you guide them through it?

Preserve Play

Play is a small child's work and an older child's refreshment. Serious illness or continuing crisis need not steal this from children. In fact, the need for play may increase. Pediatric hospitals have playrooms for a reason—as children play, they forget about their pain, express their ideas, and grow as people. Deliberately defend this crucial aspect of childhood.

Provide play wherever your child's crisis takes him. Bring a bag of fun tools along to doctor visits, speech lessons, and other appointments involving long drives or tedious waits. Include such goodies as a pad and colored pens, stickers, handcrafts, and new books.

Play not only passes the time, distracts from what's coming, and makes procedures more bearable; play enables children to prepare for and recover from medical procedures. Emily and I play hangman with words like *spinal tap, bone marrow, methotrexate, prednisone,* and other procedure and medicine names. After Erin got her braces, she and her sister applied bands and wires to every stuffed animal in the house. They played orthodontist with paper clips, rubber bands, and colored paper. When the dolls complained of symptoms remarkably similar to Erin's, Erin knew how to help.

> As children play, they forget about their pain, express their ideas, and grow as people. Deliberately defend this crucial aspect of childhood.

No matter what the procedure, ask for twin equipment to take home. I've received my share of bone marrows and spinals as Emily administers them from huge, needle-less syringes. Sarah has put me to sleep with the spare anesthesia mask her doctor sent with her after ear surgery. Emily lies perfectly still while Sarah examines her ears. I've heard both girls comfort their dolls after a rough procedure.

Love Notes

Put your concern for a family-in-crisis into action by maintaining their supply of take-along tools. Deliver these before doctor visits or during an extended hospitalization. One thoughtful friend even supplies the bag to take them in. Items you might want to include:

Travel games

Magic pen books

Videotapes of Sunday School lessons

Floss for friendship bracelets

Coloring stickers

Audiotapes of worship services

Puzzle books

Card games

Hand-held tape player

Washable markers

A checkered picnic tablecloth and a doctor-approved fun meal to serve on it

Cars or boats

Jacks and ball

Colored pens

Unique bubble gum

A photo box in which to collect cards and notes

Draw your own puzzles

Alphabet stickers

Fancy pencils with a pad to match

"Hot Loops" or other hand weaving

Music or story cassette tapes

Crossword puzzles or word searches

Books in the child's favorite series

Videotapes to watch in the middle of the night if your child can't sleep

MadLib® books

Fingernail stickers or sticker tattoos

Beads to make bracelets and necklaces

Punch-out paper dolls with an envelope to keep them in

Tiny action figures (find out your young friend's favorites)

Quarters for vending machines or cafeteria treats.

Add fun to all of these by wrapping them in pretty paper.

Bonus Resources

Sources like these can provide play tools for your child. Build a collection before you need them.

- Pediatric Projects, P.O. Box 571555, Tarzana, CA 91357-1555, 1-800-947-0947, 1-818-887-1423; publishes a catalog full of medical toys and books—including such unique items as a working stethoscope, a doll cast kit, fun bandages, a teddy bear with eye patches, arm slings, shoulder immobilizers, an ICU bed, specialty medical items, and a myriad of books. Both ill and healthy children enjoy these toys.

- Jesana, Ltd. (P.O. Box 17, Irvington, NY 10533) provides toys for children with physical challenges. Samples include hand-propelled tricycles, wheelchairs for dolls, and an audio ball for visually impaired children.

- JCPenney Special Needs Catalog. This specialty catalog available at JCPenney stores or by calling 1-800-709-5777 includes easy dressing fashions for children of all sizes and ages.

- Makit (P.O. Box 769100, Dallas TX 75376, 1-800-248-9443; www.makit.com) offers crafts such as make-your-own Christmas ornaments, picture pins, and plates. These items can be made at home or in a hospital bed.

- Department stores in your community have toy, craft, and school supply departments that can provide just what your child is looking for. Browse when things are calm and build up a stash of projects you can pull out during an emergency, illness, or simple boredom. Watch for out-of-the-ordinary items with great play value such as paper reinforcements for snowman building, office supply stickers to play post office, and blank cassette tapes for recording stories, experiences, or secret messages.

- Societies and Organizations: The American Cancer Society (1-800-4-CANCER) and other specific-to-the-crisis societies frequently provide coloring books and other play tools that both explain the illness and help children play through it. Some are free. Others are inexpensive.

- The ARC (Association for Retarded Citizens; 1-800-433-5255; www.thearc.org) provides equipping, support, and encouragement for persons challenged with mental retardation and for their families. Ask about literature, the national publication, insurance information, and more.

As an added bonus, syringes, finger bandages, and tongue depressors provide great fun when used for other than intended uses—syringes makes great water guns; bandages hold gift wrappings together for hospital gifts; tongue depressors make great log cabins and toast getter-outers. As children play with these medical instruments, they become less fearful of them. They also work out their anger about the pain they've been through—I let Emily give the roughest spinals to her teddy bears.

In addition to medical-related and getting-through-the-waiting-room-time play, build in time for your child to simply play. Hectic schedules, whether medical or routine, steal the dreaming and creating time that helps children grow. Find at least an hour every week, preferably a whole afternoon, when your child can dream and play in her own way at her own pace. Schedule time to be unscheduled.

Provide respite in the midst of the crisis when possible. Take time off from the hard times to relax, forget about the crisis for a time, build family closeness, and enjoy. Some families take a day away from town, others spend an hour together each evening, still others make hospital or recuperation time fun in a new way.

The need for play is not limited to small children. Everyone needs the refreshment that comes from free time. Your middle-schooler may like to draw or shoot baskets. Your senior-higher may like organizing his comic book collection or nurturing a garden. You may like browsing through catalogs or playing in a volleyball tournament. Everyone needs dream time and free time. Refuse to be sucked into, or let your child be sucked into, the plan-every-minute-of-your-day trap.

> Find at least an hour every week, preferably a whole afternoon, when your child can dream and play in her own way at her own pace. Schedule time to be unscheduled.

GROW FAITH

"You know, sometimes I get pretty mad at God for making my eyes this way," said Phil, a young, visually impaired child.

"I'd get real mad at Him if I thought He were the one who gave this to you," responded his father. "But the Bible assures us in 1 John 1:5 that God is light and in him is no darkness at all. God is the giver of good gifts, not bad ones. Your sight is a distortion of the good sight He created you to have. The Bible also says in James 1:16 and 17 not to be deceived, that the bad stuff doesn't come from God. It says, 'Every good and perfect gift is from ... the Father.' God doesn't like your vision problem any more than you do. That's why He helps you with it."

"Whew! Good. I didn't want to be mad at God," said Phil.

"You can be mad, but give your anger to the one who deserves it—the devil. Then tell God when you get mad or sad. He understands and will show you what to do about it," suggested Phil's father. "He's on your side to help you through both good and bad."

Crises present some ticklish faith questions, and children aren't afraid to ask them. Chapter 8 explores many of these questions. Each question your child asks provides opportunity to grow in faith and understanding. So answer questions honestly and with careful evaluation of what the Bible really says, not what you wish it said or what you've heard it says. Refuse to bless wrong assumptions like, "That little boy died because God needed another angel," or "God took that mother to be with Him." God doesn't take people away from their families. Germs, accidents, disabilities, and carelessness do that. Children don't become angels—angels are specially created beings that are neither human nor divine. Instead of using pat answers, courageously speak the truth—evil comes because of the presence of Satan and because of the imperfection of this world. Romans 8:22 describes the whole creation groaning over the bentness of this world. One day things will be perfect. But we aren't there yet.

Don't build resentment against God by letting your child believe that God gave a disease, a disability, or a crisis. As Matthew 7:9-11 explains, God wouldn't give a stone in place of bread. God knows even better than we human parents how to give good gifts. And don't assume that bad is really good, that the disease or disability is really a blessing in disguise. That's not what God teaches at all.

Instead, build togetherness with God by noticing His good gifts—hearing aids, glasses, medical treatments, good friends, and more—and by honestly assuring your child that God grieves deeply when, for instance, a drunk driver takes the life of a grandmother. This world is imperfect. And people make horrible choices that affect very innocent people. Suffering such as disabilities come from no clear cause. One day God will make everything right (Rev. 21:3-4). In the meantime, we help each other through the yuck of this life.

Childhood faith development is more than attending church and saying bedtime prayers. It's providing natural opportunities for growth. One mother shares, "While visiting a friend and overhearing her guide her son's bedtime prayer, I realized with consternation that we had no bedtime prayer at home. I worried that I wasn't providing adequate spiritual direction. My prayers are more a continuous conversation with God than a 'Now I lay me down to sleep' cap to the day. The nighttime ritual had seemed just that to me, and without meaning to I had omitted it from my son's life. Then one day Tim and I were in the car singing Bible verse songs and he said, 'This is the one I sing when Tony is mean to me at school— "Do not be overcome by evil. But overcome evil with good." When I feel like hitting him back I just keep repeating, "Overcome evil with good. Overcome evil with good." Over and over I say it.'

"I choked back tears of joy as I recognized that Tim had learned to pray. He communicated with God continually so he could live God's truth. Rather than lead bedtime prayers, I had purchased fun-to-listen-to Bible memory tapes. After reflecting on this experience, I recognized songs as one of my favorite ways to worship and grow. I'm not musical—in fact, all I can do is make a joyful noise—so I wouldn't have consciously chosen that avenue for spiritual training. But I thanked God for working through me in this unintentional way."

Remember Trish—the girl who didn't think of herself as sick? Her parents also encouraged the good God was creating in Trish. They allowed her time to study her Bible, to pray, and to think. These precious moments produced insights Trish could use in both the good and bad of life with a body cast. Her parents then worked as God's ambassadors by providing avenues for Trish to express her faith through developing friendships, through marching in the band, through finding and wearing comfortable clothes, and through keeping on keeping on.

Like Trish's, Tim's, and Phil's parents, we can simply move aside and work along with God as He brings out the childlikeness in our children. We can believe that "anyone who will not receive the kingdom of God like a little child will never enter it" (Mark 10:15).

RELIEVE WORRIES

"Children bounce back so fast."

"They handle things so much better than adults do."

"Children have nothing to worry about."

Too frequently we adults dismiss children's suffering with words like these. Certainly children are gifted with a focus on the present and a joy that pokes its way through the worst of pain. But children are not carefree. Their shots and stitches hurt just as much as adults' do. They have genuine worries about robbers, fires, monsters, and more. These worries matter. Give sincere attention to your child's worries by listening, asking questions, and discovering solutions together. Don't assume your child feels the same way you do, even when you worry about the same things. Instead, listen and watch to notice what your child feels and thinks. Guide your child to actions and information that can melt or manage her worries. Assure her that God and you want to help.

After seeing a fire on the 6:00 P.M. news, Gwen asked, "Do you think our house will burn like that, Daddy?"

"Probably not, because we're careful with matches. And that house was old and run down. But it could happen. When I'm worried about something that could, but probably won't, happen, I think about what I'd do. Then I don't worry quite as much," suggested Daddy.

"What will we do, Daddy?" asked Gwen.

Gwen's dad felt like they'd been through the escape plan at least a thousand times, but he patiently overviewed it again. "We'll get out as fast as we can and then go next door to call 911. Where do we meet?"

"The swing set," said Gwen.

"How do you get out of the house?" asked Daddy.

"Crawl, or stop-drop-and-roll," said Gwen.

"What if you leave your teddy bear behind?" asked Daddy.

"Let the fireman go back for him, not me," Gwen replied with confidence but sadness.

"Exactly," said Daddy. "What if you can't find Mama or me?"

"Just stay at the swing set, and you'll come soon," said Gwen.

"Right. 'Cause if we don't see you at the swing set, we'd worry. Go there and stay there," said Daddy.

"And you go there and stay there, too," insisted Gwen.

"We will," promised Daddy.

"But what if I'm asleep, Daddy? What if the smoke detector doesn't go off?" asked Gwen.

"If you're asleep, I'll wake you. We keep fresh batteries in the smoke detector so it will go off; but if it doesn't, we will probably wake up," explained Daddy.

"What if the fire burns us up before we can get out?" asked Gwen.

"Fires doesn't usually work that fast," said Daddy. "But if it did, you'd go to heaven."

"I'd rather stay here with you," said Gwen.

"Me, too, and I think you will," said Daddy. "You'll probably never face a fire. I never have. But you know what to do if it does happen. And knowing what to do can make you less afraid. Whenever you get your fire fear, remember our escape plan. Come here and give me a hug."

Child's Viewpoint

One difference between childhood and adult worries is the approach: Children tend to worry hard and then forget about it. They seldom dwell on problems. We adults worry before, during, and after the event. Children worry, find a solution, and move on. But until they find a solution, children feel their problems and fears intensely. They may hold their lonely fears inside. Watch for signs of worry to give the strategies, listening, and honest answers your child needs. Guide them to interpret and respond, to form a plan. Provide actions and ideas that help them manage the worry.

Talking about worries takes away much of their power. In fact Jesus encourages us to turn worries into prayer, to talk things over with Him until we know what to do (Matt. 6:33; Rom. 8:26-27). Writing, drawing, and playing help, too. These actions work out fears children can't quite put into words or don't feel like talking about. Gwen draws plentiful pictures of burning houses with family members safely outside. As she and other children write and draw, they share their feelings with God. Because you never know just when your child will need them, keep paper, pencils, diaries, notebooks, and play figures within your child's reach at all times. Your child will frequently bring her writings and drawings to you. She may also invite you to play. Treasure these gifts with, "I'm glad you trusted me with this," "Tell me about this picture," and, "How does the little girl feel?"

Childhood worries are not always over in one conversation, nor do children always reveal their worries instantly.

Six weeks after her hospitalization for initial treatment of leukemia, Emily spoke of her fears about surgery. "I didn't think I'd be afraid, but I was. I'd read all those books, but when it came to actually having an operation myself, I was scared stiff. I thought I'd wake up during the operation. I wondered if they'd start cutting before I was good and asleep. I didn't like all those people poking at me."

This revealing conversation came while Emily and I casually worked a jigsaw puzzle. I would have said that she was perfectly comfortable with the surgery, that she came through the hospitalization without a hitch, that she didn't mind the student doctors who examined her. She reminded me that crises are seldom dealt with in one blow—a hospital visit or another trauma may have to be relived over and over. I also discovered the significance of providing opportunities to talk. I had asked her several times about her feelings, but she said little. Direct questions can seem too potent. Much more successful are activities where talking can happen but is not forced—walking, working puzzles, or riding in a car. Then Emily and I are free to talk about deep questions, funny memories, lasting fears, or simple frustration over not finding the right puzzle piece. Emily can, and does, take the lead.

> Direct questions can seem too potent. Much more successful are activities where talking can happen but is not forced—walking, working puzzles, or riding in a car.

126

YOUR FEELINGS MATTER TO ME

Take your child's worries as seriously as you want yours taken. For example:

Don't Say	*Do Say*
"That's nothing to worry about."	"It probably won't happen, but what will we do if it does?"
"Don't talk that way."	"You can tell me how you feel."
"It won't hurt much."	"Yes, it will hurt, but not for long."
"You don't really mean that."	"You feel very strongly about this, don't you?"
"Just let God handle it."	"God understands your feelings. Shall we talk to Him about them now? Would you like to go first?"
"You're so brave."	"This is awful, but I know you can do it."
"It's not that bad."	"It's hard. I'm right beside you."

Ration Your Energy

Whether your crisis is a continuing handicap, an uncertain illness, or a series of daily challenges, you must provide your child with the normalcy she needs to stay in the middle of life at its fullest. This equipping takes daily inventiveness and is a wearying process that can physically and emotionally exhaust us parents. Even though the results are so worth it—a child who flourishes and enjoys the best of childhood—we get very tired.

Part of managing continuing crises with children is saving energy to do so.

Dealing day after day with my daughters' continuing crises can make me feel like I'm going under. On top of their pain, my own grief weighs me down relentlessly. I go to bed exhausted from confronting the latest hearing hurdle or agonizing over another round of chemo side effects. I'm not sure I even have the energy to fall asleep. Then the mercy of slumber demonstrates God's promise found in Lamentations 3:22-23: "Because of the Lord's great love we are not consumed, for his compassions never fail. They are new every morning; great is your faithfulness."

I awaken in the morning refreshed, conscious of God's delicious serving of compassion, specifically designed for that day. I see new reasons for joy and feel confident we will make it. Morning by morning I meet the challenges ahead. When I try to do it all at once, or even think about it at all, I panic.

Part of managing continuing crises with children is saving energy to do so. I cannot take sixteen volunteer jobs at church, keep up with my full-time job, maintain an immaculate house, stay up late, get up early, and still have time and patience to respond to my children's needs. I have to scale back and I have to do so proportionally. Dropping church or dropping work is not the answer. Instead I've got to do a little of all the things that are important in life. I have to maintain a balance in my life so I can help my children balance theirs. This balance is excruciatingly hard, especially when hours of waiting room time crowd into the other events we had planned. But we do our best. I accept one job at church, and I try to do it well. I do my writing job as completely as I can during work hours and try to avoid working late. I hire a housekeeper to clean my house biweekly and lower my standards of domestic perfection— which I must admit were pretty low already! I guard my Sunday afternoon nap religiously. I leave evenings for family and play. I set an early weeknight bedtime so I can get up in time to get the girls unhurriedly to school by 7:30 A.M. I'm often worn out by 8:00 P.M.

I'm convinced that another reason I've been able to keep going in the face of continuing pain is that my family hibernates. Following a round of chemotherapy, we get substitutes for our regular activities and pull together as a family to just be. These times of decreased circulation and huddling give us the refreshment and healing we need to return to life.

Even with everything scaled back and even with periods of rest, I do things more slowly and less efficiently when my children are in crisis. Though I'm impatient with this, I'm learning to live with it. I know my usual tasks will take longer, and I try to set my deadlines and commitments accordingly. Each time we go for a chemo or checkup visit,

I think I'll manage it fine—after all, Emily is in remission and things are going well. But it wipes me out every time. I have to allow room for recovery. I've got to accept fatigue and sadness as godly responses to pain, and refuse to feel guilty about these very healthy responses.

Friends are the final factor that make it possible to get through these deeply painful times. After Emily was diagnosed with leukemia, I could not keep up my weekly commitment at church. Because one week in four is filled with the family-wide agony of chemotherapy, I had to miss every fourth Sunday. Rather than drop all service, I found a friend willing to be a regular substitute. Her genuine care for my Youth Sunday School class made me feel my class was in good hands. She made it possible for me to keep serving. Without the refreshment that comes from giving to others, I would have languished. Without the consistent break my caring friend gave, I would have neglected my class.

Love Notes

Be the friend who understands that continuing crises aren't over when a child returns to routine life. Keep in touch with your friend. Ask how it's going and then listen to the details. Substitute for her jobs at church or school, or find someone who can do so. Find out what other regular jobs need doing and help with them. Ask what you can specifically pray for, such as energy on that rough day or a caring teacher to help the child through an important milestone. Write significant dates on your calendar. Walk with your friend without pushing. Be there in person or online, be open, be hopeful, be responsive.

Thankfully, not all families face continuing crises. Most crises come unexpectedly and briefly, challenging us to respond lovingly and in ways that produce growth. Accidents and emergency room visits, fights with friends, and lost homework require steadiness and quick thinking. They also require us to go on with life. With God's power, mercy, and creativity we can do exactly that. Following an emergency room visit, we give our children play syringes, stitches, casts, and bandages so they can play through the experience. Their play equips them to face the next crisis without panic. After a fight with a friend, our children list words and actions to mend the rift without a scar. We then support them as they try those words and actions. When they lose their homework, we assure our children that everyone makes mistakes and then suggest they keep their work in a notebook so it's always there when they need it.

> Even a lifelong challenge is made up of a series of small ones. Facing these one by one and with God's daily measure of grace, we find steadiness, love, and energy to redeem our children's crises and to live the joy.

Even a lifelong challenge is made up of a series of small ones. Facing these one by one and with God's daily measure of grace, we find steadiness, love, and energy to redeem our children's crises and to live the joy.

THE POINT ⟵

Children experience the world in a unique and lovely way. When they encounter crises, we fear all this loveliness will be lost. But this fear need not become reality. In the midst of a new experience, accident, handicap, or illness, our children can, and should, enjoy all that is good about childhood. Help this happen by preserving family, play, and faith, by helping through worries, and by taking the time to enjoy life.

Chapter 7

Work Closely with the School

"It's not that I felt strong or especially gifted, I just didn't want to miss anything. I stayed in the hospital frequently and went through incredible pain, but I don't feel like I missed life."
—Adult recalling her childhood battle with scoliosis of the spine

One fall our Sarah had tube surgery to prevent the ear infections that further decrease her hearing. For three very long weeks she could wear only one hearing aid and had great difficulty hearing. Her second-grade teacher kept Sarah closer than usual, repeated class comments when necessary, wrote all instructions, and went the extra mile to be certain Sarah understood every happening in the classroom. Best of all, this teacher did not consider these actions an imposition. "That's just the way it is, and we'll find a way to manage it," she said. I wanted to hug her.

This teacher's attitude was so loving and supportive that Sarah made it through that incredibly frustrating time without a hitch. Teachers like this are wonderful gifts. They impart and live the joy in life. Through tears I wrote her a note of thanks. Words seemed inadequate to express my gratitude. I prayed she would understand how much she meant to me and to Sarah.

How can all children in crisis have this kind of positive experience at school? We've found working as a team and expressing appreciation to be the two most important factors in continuing a good school experience. As you and the teacher work together to share information, to support each other's goals, and to bring out the best in your child, everyone benefits.

> We've found working as a team and expressing appreciation to be the two most important factors in continuing a good school experience.

This team process involves information sharing, mutual problem-solving, and continual communication. Bathe all these in expressed appreciation. Teachers are people first and, like all people, they grow through thanks for what they do well rather than criticism for where they blunder. Timely notes, words of specific thanks, balloons delivered to home or school, birthday surprise parties, hand-picked flowers, and simple gifts on non-holidays remind your child's teacher of her talents and your gratitude. Work toward developing genuine and mutual friendships with your children's teachers.

SELECT GOOD TEACHERS

Foundational to working as a team is choosing the right teacher in the first place. The teacher who works with your child daily helps him walk through his challenges and interprets the crisis to friends. Some teachers are better at this close contact and compassionate caring than others. One might worry so much that she makes your child anxious and uneasy. Another may disregard the problem, causing your child to miss significant amounts of classroom instruction. Still another may baby or pamper your child, refuse to discipline, and consequently build resentment among classmates. A teacher may see special needs as a bother, communicating this resentment to your child and causing your child to wonder

> Seek the critical balance between modification and high expectation, between compassion and discipline, between taking the crisis seriously and overreacting.

why his teacher doesn't like him. Seek the critical balance between modification and high expectation, between compassion and discipline, between taking the crisis seriously and overreacting. One parent told of a teacher who was perfect for one child but disastrous with the other. It's not that one teacher is good and another bad. We simply need the right match for our children.

Check with former teachers who worked well with your child and can confidentially recommend personalities who would blend with your child's. Before classes are assigned, ask the principal to select a teacher who can meet your child's needs. (See the section later in this chapter for ideas on crises that hit midyear). Together, find a teacher sensitive to and gifted in meeting the specific needs of your child. Our Sarah needs a teacher with an easy-to-hear voice and an expressive face, a teacher who doesn't mind wearing the FM transmitter that aids hearing in the classroom, who uses plentiful visuals, who has high expectations, and who naturally finds creative ways to communicate.

PUT YOUR THANKFULNESS INTO WORDS

- Steven can finally tell time, thanks to you. He has struggled for years but your methods make time crystal clear. Thanks.

- Erin comes home repeating your lessons word for word. You are obviously communicating beautifully.

- Thanks for making that adjective lesson so interesting! Fernando's still looking for adjectives that fit the letters of his name.

- Just about the time my son got spring fever, you added the "Wonderful Wednesdays." Thanks for keeping school interesting.

- I really appreciate the way your art projects relate to academics. Through this approach you gave Cassie opportunity to learn more and to express what she has already learned.

- Your daily journal is wonderful. And the stories the children write and self-edit are great. Through these activities Shanna is learning self-expression and clear communication. Thanks!

DEVELOP A LEARNING PLAN FOR YOUR CHILD

Once a teacher has been selected, meet with this chosen teacher to discover ways to equip your child to master her challenges. This give-and-take process is precious beyond measure when it works well. Children face some challenges that are consistent, others that change with each new year.

This process occurs during casual meetings and in many schools during a formal M-Team meeting (see "Bonus Resources" box). Together, past and present teachers, principals, specialists specific to your child's needs, and you the parent generate a list of actions that will help your child learn while not setting her apart. This individualized education plan is carried out during the school year.

Bonus Resources

Children in the US with handicapping conditions are entitled to a free public education in the least restrictive environment according to a federal law called Public Law 94-142. In most cases this means attending public school with modifications. The law states that a multidisciplinary team (M-Team) will get together to plan an Individualized Education Program (IEP) for the child. Contact your local school system or your state Department of Education for more information and to learn if your child qualifies.

As the team develops a learning plan and shares casual information, previous experiences give way to present accuracies. Teachers discover that children with profound hearing loss can talk and listen clearly in a regular classroom. Parents discover that the teacher uses visuals to make learning easier for all pupils.

As teachers and parents pool ideas for solving or working around the crisis, uncertainty gives way to specific caring—parents of a learning disabled student suggest math strategies that have helped their son master addition in the past. Teachers share new strategies they will use this year. Teachers, parents, and administrators continue to work together during the year in an invaluable partnership that gives the child the best of both home and school.

SHARE INFORMATION

Share information not only with the teacher and principal but also with the "hub" of the school. Who is the hub? The person to whom people go for the inside scoop, the one they ask when they feel shy about asking you. In our elementary school she's the school secretary who serves as nurse, mama, and problem solver. In our middle school, the hub is the school counselor. Talk with this person every time something changes in your child's status and ask her to be your liaison for communicating information to and from you.

We summarize the information and ideas generated in our M-Team (see "Bonus Resources" box) and give them to anyone who has a teaching role with our daughter. We try to strike a balance between providing enough specifics to be helpful while keeping the list short enough to be read.

Sharing information also requires a delicate balance between "She's OK," so people won't panic and "Here's what to watch for," so people can take good care of your child during critical times. It's a balance between "He's just like you," so he won't be set apart from the group and "Here are the needs," so he can get the most from classroom instruction.

SAMPLE LEARNING PLAN

We want that delicate balance of meeting Sarah's hearing needs while not setting her apart from the rest of the class. Rather than excuse her for not hearing, make sure she understands you. Sarah has severe hearing loss which means that she begins hearing at 70 decibels (normal speech is at 50). We don't know the cause of her hearing loss. We do know that it is nerve deafness, is permanent (barring a miracle), and is greatly helped with hearing aids. With hearing aids, she has a mild loss. This means that in the classroom she hears about 87 percent when she can see the faces of all who are talking. She has the most trouble when several people talk at once, when the words sound alike ("sand" and "tan"), or when the idea is new. Ways to prevent misunderstanding or to clear it up once it has occurred include:

• Let Sarah sit in the desk closest to the teacher. Distance and noise are her biggest enemies, so be close when possible. If necessary, talk directly into her ear.

- Direct your voice and face to Sarah when convenient. Talk normally and assume she hears you unless she says otherwise.

- Wear an auditory trainer microphone. This FM system brings the sound of your voice or AV equipment right to Sarah's ear. You (or the VCR) wear a clip microphone connected to a device about the size of a pocket radio. Sarah wears the receiver in loop form (like a necklace) connected to a device the size of a radio. She wears a belt or uses her jeans. She keeps an extra belt for you. Past teachers have used aprons.

- Be matter-of-fact about her hearing loss. Rather than call her "special," please just say her ears don't work and she must do all she can to hear and understand.

- Clarify similar sounding words by spelling them or giving a sentence. Because some letters sound alike (f and s; b and d; e and v; m and n), "fan" sounds like "sand." So when talking about "sand," say, "It starts with 's' like Sarah, not 'f' like freckle."

- Please give sentences for all spelling tests.

- Rephrase. If she doesn't understand the first time, say it a different way. (E.g.: "A noun is a person, place, or thing" or "A noun is a thing the sentence tells about.")

- Let her read your lips when she needs to. Sarah's hearing is strong enough that she doesn't always need to read lips. But when her hearing is down due to a cold or ear infection, when the situation is noisy, or when the voice is quiet, she reads lips. Don't exaggerate or slow your speech.

- Like all children, sometimes Sarah asks, "What?" when she doesn't understand a concept, not because she can't hear you. Please explain the concept to her or say it in a different way.

- Place tennis balls on the feet of all classroom chairs to muffle chair noise. Cut down on other classroom noise where possible. The hearing aids pick up the loudest sounds, not the most important.

- Let her ask questions or explain back to you. Feel free to say, "Can you hear me all right?" or "Does this make sense?" She is comfortable talking about her hearing difficulties. Assume she hears you if she doesn't say otherwise—she is very good at letting you know.

- Maintain her hearing aids and FM system. Sarah's hearing aids are relatively maintenance free. She keeps a spare battery. The trainer has instructions on the box. If there are problems with the hearing aids or trainer that Sarah can't solve, please send her to the office to call me. (I can come to school or advise over the phone.)

- Please believe the best about Sarah and guide her over rough spots to success. Expect and enforce good behavior, kind attitudes and actions, attentive work, eager learning. When something is hard, teach her how to do it rather than excuse her for not doing it.

- Because people learn to talk through hearing, Sarah's speech is occasionally unclear. When you (or a student) don't understand her, explain that you didn't understand and ask her to say it more slowly or in a different way (or encourage the student to do this). She's been in speech training since infancy, and we continue to use a preventive coupled with remedial approach. Please let the speech teacher know areas we need to focus on.

- Persons who can provide information or tips for doing the above include:

  _____ ___, Teacher of the Hearing Impaired
  (phone number)
  _____ ___, Audiologist (phone number)
  _____ ___, Special Education Supervisor (phone number)
  _____ ___, Parents (phone number)

BUILD A TEAM EVEN WITHOUT THE FORMALITIES

Not every student can work from an IEP, the document that makes the education plan legally binding. The father of a twelve-year-old shares, "The general label for her is 'learning disabled.' The problem is that in repeat testing she tested OK, so we're no longer legally entitled to get help. This is extremely discouraging because we know she can't make it unassisted in the classroom. Her need for individual direction did not show up during the test, possibly because the tester worked with her individually.

"Sometimes she cries when doing homework. Last night she was thinking so hard she started shaking. She was frustrated because she couldn't grasp how to do it, and we were frustrated because we had explained and explained and didn't know how to make it any clearer. We know it's a perceptual difficulty, but no one can put a finger on it."

Is this family doomed? Not at all. Though it is not defined, the learning disability is real. This father can follow almost all of the same steps without the formal structure the law provides for qualifying children. He can develop friendships with teachers, share what has worked and hasn't worked in the past, provide written information, thank teachers for the good things they do, and work as part of a team to solve each challenge. These actions are crucial to the success of any learning plan, and with the right teacher, work just as effectively without a legally mandated IEP.

This same strategy works well for shorter-term crises such as a brief illness or the death of a grandparent:

- Share what has happened.
- List together what will help your child though it.
- Communicate continually to keep meeting other needs that arise.
- Bathe it all in appreciation and mutuality.

WATCH HOW YOU SAY IT

I've found it extremely important to watch my attitude during preparation for a new school year or problem solving during the school year. I'm a strong-willed person by nature, and I become even more intense when my children are at stake. Though I never mean to come across forcefully, I've discovered the hard way that I have approached teachers with information that came across as orders rather than suggestions. I've assumed I know my children and their needs best but, though this may frequently be true, teachers know about areas I don't. I must balance my advocacy efforts with patience and respect. I need to learn from the teacher as well as invite him to learn from me. One teacher told me to back off. Another took it out on my child.

These few sad experiences have reminded me to be sensitive rather than supervisory, appreciative rather than demanding, open to advice rather than certain of what needs to be done, cooperative rather than insistent. I've learned to ask for ideas rather than come with a preset plan.

At the same time, I hasten to add that teachers do appreciate information and help. Unless a friend or family member has been through a particular crisis, it's unlikely they'll know much about it. When we suspected hearing loss in our infant, I remarked to the nurse with whom I was making an appointment, "I don't imagine there is any rush to see the doctor because I don't guess they can do anything for bad hearing."

> I've discovered the hard way that I have approached teachers with information that came across as orders rather than suggestions.

"Certainly we can do something," she said. "We'd fit her with hearing aids."

"A baby?" I remarked in return. Although hearing aids made perfect sense once I heard the suggestion, I'd never thought about using hearing aids with a child. I'd seen them only on senior adults.

CREATE A HAPPY BEGINNING

As you prepare for a new school year or adjust to a crisis that lands in the middle of the year, do the detail work that makes for a successful school experience. Parents of children in crisis compiled this list:

- *Take your child to meet the teacher ahead of time.* Whether in elementary, middle, or high school this breaks the ice for both teacher and student. It also banishes any prejudices or preset expectations. Both teacher and student will know each other on the first day of school or will have talked things over before the first day back after a crisis. Your child will feel like he has an advocate, and the teacher will feel comfortable meeting his needs. Ask the teacher to set a convenient time for this.

- *Give printed information.* What should the teacher do when your child has a seizure? How would you like him to explain her epilepsy to the class? How often do seizures tend to come? Does anything specific set them off or warn of their approach? What have former teachers said or done that has been effective? What has hurt? What else do you want your child's teacher to know?

- *Overview any equipment.* How does your child's asthma inhaler work? What's the best way to get the wheelchair down the stairs? How does a line marker help your child read more effectively?

- *Share how it all impacts school.* Does the elusive learning disability get worse under certain circumstances? What's the best way to learn in spite of it? How does your child feel about the learning disability? What actions have helped or hurt in the past?

- *Stress that your child is a hard worker.* Too many students use their IEPs as excuses not to do their work. Explain that your child wants to learn, and will work diligently.

- *Determine the best time and ways to communicate.* Some teachers like notes; some like phone calls; some like you to drop by before or after school; some prefer talking from home rather than school. Ask your teacher's preference and comply with her wishes.

- *Ask if your teacher will tell you her birthday and home address.* Then send a card on her birthday or request school permission to give a surprise party. Mail get-well cards when your child's teacher is sick or send cookies when she's done something especially helpful. Encourage your child to make or help make these treats.

- *Give your phone number(s) and address.* Assure your teacher that you can be at the school within minutes or offer as much availability as you can. Let the teacher know where to reach you twenty-four hours a day. If you are frequently away from the phone, let your teacher know how to get messages to you. Offer names and numbers of medical personnel, relatives, or others who can help interpret or solve predicaments.

- *Work toward that delicate balance between understanding your child's crisis and not treating her differently.* Let everything you do work toward good learning and good citizenship. Equip your child to give more than he receives.

Manage Midyear Problems

When a crisis hits midyear, you don't have the luxury of selecting and preparing with your child's teacher. Mrs. Underwood absolutely freaked out when Derek returned to school after being diagnosed with cancer. For three days in a row she sent him home. First she said, "I didn't like his color." Next she said, "He looked tired." Then she said,

"He had trouble concentrating." The fourth day, a former teacher found Derek crying outside the classroom before school. Derek said Mrs. Underwood yelled at him every day, and he didn't want to go in.

Derek's father was furious that Derek's eight-year-old classmates handled his illness better than a grown woman. After getting his anger in check, he contacted Mrs. Underwood to discover the problem. Derek's dad explained that Derek was ready for full days at school and asked what they could do to help things go more smoothly. He repeated the previously conveyed information from Derek's doctor that the cancer was in remission, that Derek could resume normal activities, and that if he got tired to let him lay his head on the desk.

Mrs. Underwood had little to say. So Derek's father went to the principal. He calmly explained what had happened over the past several days. The principal revealed Mrs. Underwood's conviction that Derek would be better with a homebound teacher. He assured Derek's father that he would do whatever he could for Derek, that Derek was welcome at school, but that maybe he would be better off at home.

Derek's father promptly called the doctor, who repeated his insistence that Derek be in school. After the principal heard the doctor's recommendation, he talked with Mrs. Underwood, explaining that there was no reason to recommend Derek stay with a homebound teacher. Derek was expected to recover fully, and part of that recovery was to continue his schooling.

The next several weeks were tense ones for Mrs. Underwood and confusing ones for Derek. He didn't understand the change in his previously well-liked teacher.

As it turned out, Mrs. Underwood's mother had died

from cancer in four short months after she was diagnosed. Apparently she feared Derek would die too, perhaps in her classroom. She let hurt over her own crisis keep her from helping Derek with his.

When a crisis hits in the middle of a school year, work with the teacher and the principal to make the transitions smooth. If all else fails, you may have to change teachers or schools. Let your child's needs be paramount, balanced with equipping him to deal with the imperfect people who inhabit our imperfect world.

USE THE POWER OF THE BLESSING

Even more important than your work with school officials is your relationship with your child. Equip him to handle the daily challenges he faces with words of blessing. Words of blessing not only equip your child to deal with crises but also ward off future problems. A child who enters school feeling loved will act cooperatively, will show kindness to friends and will attack assignments more competently.

Work toward making each day a good one. While your child dresses, eats breakfast, or heads

> Words of blessing not only equip your child to deal with crises but also ward off future problems. A child who enters school feeling loved will act cooperatively, show kindness to friends, and attack assignments more competently.

out the door, use words of blessing to communicate your confidence in him and your hope for this new day. Save words of discipline or tough problem solving for later in the day. No matter how many people or problems have put him down recently, you can be on his side (see Jesus' blessing in Mark 10:13-16).

Love Notes

Ask a parent of a child in continuing crisis how school is going. Offer to pray for specific areas and help make those prayers a reality. Ways to help include:

- Pray for the selection of a teacher or the solution to a problem.
- Help the child master a specific subject.
- Transport work home from school to a homebound student, including news from school.
- Assist the child with homework or assist siblings while the parent works with the child.
- Accompany your friend to an IEP meeting.
- Listen while your friend tells the details of the latest challenge.

Think of all the ways to say "you can do it" and "this is a new and good day." Personalize this list to meet the unique needs of your child:

- "I'm proud that you woke up sweetly and got ready on time."

- "It's a new day full of good things to come."
- "I hope the spelling test goes well."
- "I'll be praying with you as you and your friends work out the lunch table dilemma."
- "I remember how well you did last time."
- "This problem has certainly been a tough one. I'm proud of the way you're managing it and keeping your friendships strong at the same time."
- "I know you'll concentrate hard and cooperate. That will help you forget your pain and help the day pass more happily."
- "You're good with colors. You'll design a great set."
- "You're a caring person. I know you'll solve the problem."
- "If the book's not in your locker when you check again, ask if you can buy another."
- "It'll be hard, but give it your best."
- "You've prepared well. I know that will help."
- "You have the speaking skills to communicate well.
- "I'm behind you all the way. I know you can do it."

Blessings are especially important during times of crisis because your child may have more than the usual difficulty separating from you. Assure him: "It won't be long until we see each other. Give me a big kiss that will last me all day. Here's one for you." Your junior-higher may not feel comfortable with public displays of affection, so give your hug and encouragement before leaving the house.

Of course, you don't need to limit your words of blessing to morning. As your child meets each challenge, whether coping with crisis or mastering a milestone, blend words of encouragement with the rough words. Your love and support can empower your child to handle anything.

THE POINT ⟵

School isn't everything—I'm a firm believer in the centrality of the home—but it's a very important thing. Continued school involvement offers the normalcy our children need to grow up whole and happy. Through school, children discover and develop skills, learn to relate to peers, thrive under marvelous teachers, and build coping skills under not-so-marvelous teachers. Whether your child attends a public school, private school, or home school, work as a team with school personnel to help your child master school during both short-term and continuing crises. Then blend play and family time around school to keep your child happily growing.

Chapter 8

Answer Questions Honestly

*"God, not the explanations about Him,
gets me through the pain."*
—Parent of a child with cancer

Why is it so long and hard?" asked my Emily during a grueling seven-day round of chemotherapy.

"I don't know," I answered as I hugged her. "But I know we'll make it through somehow. Only two more days now, and these days are the worst of the seven."

Emily's "why?" was a plea for an end to the pain, not a request for a theological discourse. I tried to assure her of that end. Because we'd been through it before, I knew approximately when she'd start to feel better.

Children are fearlessly honest in their questions. They boldly ask questions we adults fear saying out loud. "How can such a terrible thing happen to such a wonderful person?" "Why does our family have both cancer and hearing loss?" "Why did God make me this way?"

The way we handle our children's questions profoundly affects how they handle their crises. If we say God gives cancer, our children will wonder why God hurt them. They won't be likely to turn to God for help or comfort. But if we answer that cancer is a part of this imperfect world, a part that delights Satan, our children will fight the disease with God's help. They can direct their anger against Satan rather than wonder if it's OK to be mad at God. Give your child the freedom to turn to God rather than wonder why He hurt them, the freedom to hate evil rather than call it good, the freedom to move past pain to find joy in the midst of crisis.

Knowing the answers is not as important as accepting the questions. There is much we parents don't understand, and it's OK to admit that to our children. It's not OK to avoid or push aside our children's questions just because we don't know how to answer them. Refuse to fear the big questions or avoid the sticky issues. If we evade questions, our children will conclude that questions are somehow bad. They'll then hold their lonely fears inside. Accept questions to diffuse your children's fears, to help them know their feelings make sense, and to search for answers together. Let them know their questions are good ones. Even when you don't discover complete answers, assure your child that the answers are there and it's never wrong to ask. God will help us understand either in this life or the next one: "Ask and it will be given to you; seek and you will find; knock and the door will be opened to you" (Matt. 7:7).

This chapter explores sample questions from children in crisis. Each question is followed by a brief answer for a child and then a more detailed exploration of the facts behind that answer. Use both portions to voice answers that fit your child's questions and vocabulary. Let the Bible speak to both you and your child as you seek, discover, and live God's answers.

WHY DID GOD MAKE ME THIS WAY?

"God is as sad about your hearing loss as we are. God doesn't like it, so He helps us cope with it. He works with doctors and inventors to find ways to cure hearing loss and to invent tinier and better working hearing aids. And He promises us perfect bodies when we get to heaven."

I'm absolutely convinced that God does not make childhood disabilities, nor does He send illnesses to children. Disabilities and illnesses are not gifts for special families or rewards for strong faith. They're insults to God's perfectly created bodies, results of living in this imperfect world, distortions of God's good. Matthew 7:9-11 assures us:

"Which of you, if his son asks for bread, will give him a stone? Or if he ask for a fish, will give him a snake? If you, then, though you are evil, know how to give good gifts to your children, how much more will your Father in heaven give good gifts to those who ask him!"

God is the giver of good gifts, not destructive ones (see also James 1:17). He no more orchestrates a child's crippling arthritis than a human father would give his child a snake. Revelation 12:17 reminds us that the devil is hopping mad at God and is throwing a grand tantrum here on earth, attacking people every way he can. Knowing Satan is responsible for the havoc assures me that ultimately God will triumph. Knowing I don't have to be mad at God frees me to depend on Him. It assures me I can talk with Him about my anger. It also frees me to appreciate the good and fight the evil. Rather than wait until big events happen to give God credit, I can enjoy God's routine gifts, gifts like happy children and trouble-free days. I can let the tragedies be exactly that. Tragedies are interruptions to all that is good. They are thieves in the John 10:10 sense. There is no good reason for them. But God can give good in spite of them. Turn to God for help with tragedies. Don't insult God by calling tragedies gifts or assume He gave them to get your attention.

Disabilities and illnesses are not gifts for special families or rewards for strong faith. They are results of living in this imperfect world—distortions of God's good.

God created a very good world, but the human race has messed it up royally. Human greed, irresponsibility, and refusal to look further than personal comfort have created a world where people kill people, where air and water are so polluted that they cause disease, and where precious babies suffer and die. This breaks God's heart even more than it breaks ours.

We live in an imperfect world. But God didn't do it. Crises are not a testing of faith as much as an encounter with evil. Let's put the blame where it belongs. Let's stop calling bad good. And let's allow God to cry with us and help us fix the problems. His arms are ready to support us. His power can fight the pain and evil. His love assures us that one day the sadness will end:

"And God shall wipe away all tears from their eyes; and there shall be no more death, neither sorrow, nor crying, neither shall there be any more pain: for the former things are passed away" (Rev. 21:4 KJV).

But Why Did God Let It Happen? Why Doesn't He Fix It?

"I don't know. It appears to have something to do with not jumping in every time something goes wrong, something to do with freedom, something to do with letting us prevent and fix our own problems. But be assured that it's not what God likes. So He keeps on giving the good things He does like. God won't let this hearing loss get in the way of life. He continues to give you good gifts like the blue ribbon, your friendship with Gretchen, and more. These are God's gifts, not the hearing loss."

Of course, the ultimate question remains: even though Satan, a single human choice, or a series of human choices is responsible for your child's crisis, God let it happen. Why? It's true that God knows about every event. But it doesn't match His character to sit in heaven and say, "I think I'll allow Julie a bit of cancer today and Jason a car wreck." The Bible communicates His allowing as more broad—allowing all to have choices, all to choose paths, all to go certain places. And in the process of that going and choosing, some cause pain, and others run into pain. God would love to stop the pain, but for a time, He restrains

Himself. One reason is freedom; without it we are mere robots. With it we can choose genuine love, real friendship, and solid family commitment. Another reason might be the ability to find joy in the midst of pain—a demonstration that God, not circumstances, is the source of happiness.

Even so, why doesn't God stop the pain of children? Couldn't He heal a few diseases or prevent a few disabilities for His people? As we search for answers to the problem of innocent pain, we unfairly characterize God at two extremes:

• We see God as the absolute determiner of every event. Thus He must be responsible for the sad as well as the glad. We rationalize that maybe bad is really good and sad is really happy or we see God as totally uninvolved. He created the world, set it in motion, and now has little to do with what happens.

• We reason that God helps those who help themselves and that He is too busy to bother with our little problems.

I contend that God's involvement is somewhere between these extremes, expressing the best elements of both. He did indeed create the world and then gave us choices in how things would turn out. But He does not leave us to flounder like fish out of water. Even before we ask, He works to direct our choices toward good. God's influence is not pushy or coercive, or we wouldn't have true choice. But it is pervasive and thorough. God weaves and works His power in ways that allow us freedom and show His loving guidance at the same time. We can't always identify the particular "hows" and "whens" of God's guidance. But we can be certain He is alive and moving in our lives and our children's lives. This involvement is God's gift; the illness, disability, or crisis is not.

How do you see God's influence in your child's crisis? The leukemia my Emily fights now has a 75-80 percent cure rate. The cure rate was 70 percent when she began chemotherapy three years ago and will likely be higher by the time you read this book. Could God be behind the dedicated men and women who painstakingly test one chemical combination after another to discover just the formula to halt this deadly disease? I think so.

Is God the creative force behind the technological refinements that produce continuously better hearing aids for my Sarah and other children with hearing loss? Is He the motivator for the research that has produced cochlear implants and may one day cure nerve deafness? I think so.

God's gifts are not the pain, the diseases, the disabilities, the accidents. His gifts are the medicines, the hearing aids, the leg braces, the supportive families, the loyal friends, the hope for an even better future. God is actively working to end the evil in this world.

Even more reassuring is the realization that God's good is not yet complete. Three of Emily's friends with cancer have died over the last two years. Many more children died before successful chemotherapy combinations were discovered. Their mamas and daddies prayed just as fervently for their recoveries as did the parents of children who live. God doesn't like this. It breaks His tender heart. So bit-by-bit He works to conquer the evil in this world. God could squash evil like a pesky mosquito. But for reasons understood only by God, He allows Satan to rule in this world for a time. Then God steadily and persistently teaches us how to overcome that evil. He guides us to find cures. He helps us work around the disabilities. He helps us find joy in each precious day of a life cut short. He offers us certain hope of future perfection and reunion with the people who have died but continue to be so dear to us (Rom. 8:18-25; Rev. 21:4).

This hope gets us through the present pain. My Sarah's hearing aids only approximate what a human ear can do. She misses a great deal of the conversations, sounds of nature, and music in God's beautiful world. Much of this missing happens in church, during worship, during Bible teaching. This breaks my heart, and it breaks God's heart. I wish the cure was available now, but it's not. While we wait for the completion of God's good gift, Sarah and I find strategies to hear and understand, ways to live and enjoy.

The present pain is complicated by the very real fact that the ones who suffer often don't deserve it. One friend who died of cancer did everything right. She cared for other children; she kept a good attitude; she continued to serve God. But the cancer killed her in less than a year. Others who have no appreciation for life, or love, or people live long and healthy lives. It's not fair.

Here's another example of unfairness: countless persons have been hurt through the human creation of slavery. It's clearly wrong for one human being to claim to own another. But prior to the American Civil War, Christians held slaves with apparently clear consciences. They even used the Bible to support their actions. Feel the agony that enslaved parents must have felt when their children and spouses were torn from their arms and sold to other slave owners. Picture a lifetime of waiting for reunion with missing family members, realizing your yearning would likely not be satisfied this side of heaven. Why didn't God do something? I think He did.

Could God have been the One who planted the abolition

idea in leaders like Abraham Lincoln? Did God guide the Underground Railroad that secretly and nonviolently guided slave after slave to freedom? Could God have motivated the efforts that eventually granted freedom to slaves? Does God work today in people who choose friendship rather than prejudice? Is God the One who makes us colorblind? I know He is. I'm certain that God is behind every good gift for two reasons. First, the Bible says so. Second, I've seen it in my experience and the experiences of others I care about.

Even when we know without a doubt that God is alive and active in human lives, we can't box Him neatly or declare exactly how He will work. His creative, healing, and supportive forces work far beyond, and far better than, our expectations. And He works according to a timetable that surpasses our lifetimes. It took many generations to abolish slavery, and we still have a long way to go before we eradicate the prejudice that fed it. It has taken decades to come close to conquering the horror of cancer, and one in three persons still face it. We're not even close to healing paralysis, brain damage, or hearing loss. Why doesn't God work more quickly? Why don't we people learn more quickly? I don't know. In time all these diseases will pass away, and we'll have perfectly working bodies. But in the meantime too many people suffer and die. So we care for one another in every way we can think of, calling on God for ideas and power.

A WORD ABOUT "WHY?"

"Why is my son the one with cancer when he has such a brilliant brain, a loving spirit, a persistent dedication to

God? Why not someone who hates learning, who attacks people, who ignores God?"

"Why do we have to spend countless hours driving to hospitals and waiting for appointments? We have jobs and other children demanding our time. Why not someone who's bored and has nothing on the agenda but watching soap operas?"

"Why did my child die when I didn't even consume an aspirin during pregnancy? Mothers who drink, take drugs, and don't care about the children they carry, give birth to live babies and then abandon them in the hospital. It just doesn't seem fair."

"Why" questions are a plea to take away the pain, as well as a quest for answers. When we say, "Why me?" we don't really want to give the problem to someone else; we just want it to go away.

The good news is that the pain will stop. In some cases we have to wait until heaven, but the pain will end. More important than the presence of disease, disability, and death is a God who conquered all three. First Peter 5:6-11 assures us that after we have suffered a little while, God will restore us and make us strong, firm, and steadfast.

More important are questions like, "What now?" and "How do we handle this?" Because our world is imperfect and because the rain falls on good and bad alike, the distribution of crises is not always fair. But all the whys in the world won't make them go away. So we must face each crisis head-on, confident that God will empower us to make it through whatever comes (Phil. 4:13,19). As my nine-year-old says, "We'll outsmart that devil yet. He thinks he can get me down, but we'll show him!"

WHY DID THIS HAPPEN TO ME?

"I don't know why this happened to you, but I do know that good and bad happen to everyone (Matt. 5:45). God didn't single you out for this, nor has it happened because you were good or bad. The Bible explains in 1 Peter 4:12 that it's not unusual for painful things to happen in this world. Rather than worry about why something happens, let's concentrate on doing good in spite of it" (1 Pet. 4:19).

We seldom ask why good things happen to us. But we ask intensely about the bad. Though God offers glimpses of how and why He acts as He does, only He fully understands His plans. I do know we're more than pawns in an intergalactic game. And I do know that God hurts along with us when sad things happen.

We do God a disservice by trying to pinpoint exactly how He works. We must be cautious about speaking for God with words like, "This is God's will." Many are convinced that each event is God's will because God is in control. But many things happen in this world that are not God's perfect will. The Bible is full of people who disobeyed God and His will for them, making God both sad and angry. This disobedience continues today. God watches gang members attack innocent victims, but He certainly doesn't like it. He sees car

> It's not unusual for painful things to happen in this world. Rather than worry about why something happens, let's concentrate on doing good in spite of it.

accidents cripple children, but He doesn't orchestrate them.

If we say something is God's will, we must carefully define what we mean. God's will has many facets, two of which are His perfect will and His permissive will. I understand that God's perfect will includes constant obedience and loyalty from every person on earth. God wants no one to go to hell, no one to suffer debilitating disease, no one to die and be separated from family members. But love, loyalty, and obedience must be voluntary to be real. So God set His permissive will into action: He wills that we make our own choices. God allows His perfect will to be frustrated for the sake of his permissive will. In that process, God permits us to choose actions that create disease and disabilities, to choose attitudes that divide friendships rather than grow them, and to choose paths that mar the world and produce innocent suffering, some with no clear cause.

Our human choices determine much of what happens in this world. People choose to carelessly set off the firecrackers that blind and burn. People choose the mocking and rejection that lead to a friend's suicide. People design the factories that destroy healthy environments. Even so, the connections between our actions and particular sufferings aren't always clear—a carefully healthy parent is in no way responsible for the cerebral palsy that cripples her baby. This world bears the brunt of others' sinful choices and has become an unsafe place to live. God doesn't like the imperfection and He works to redeem it. When people choose to betray God's perfect will, God does not give up—He continually works to draw out the best in spite of bad circumstances and to bring people back to right choices. He invites us to work alongside Him: "All this is from God, who reconciled us to himself through Christ and gave us the ministry of reconciliation" (2 Cor. 5:18).

We can choose the encouraging word, the loving action, and the effort that leads to cure or help. We can let God use our hands to bring about the good He has in mind. We can be the source of healing and solution, rather than the one who chooses to drink. We can be the one who recycles rather than fills the land with junk. We can be the one who bridges differences rather than fears handicaps.

God doesn't like crises, nor does He give them. Instead He works in and around them to poke in good. God has made my Sarah a confident and happy child, gifts independent of her hearing loss. He has given my Emily skillful nurses who make painful procedures as easy as possible and who then take a break to celebrate that the bone marrow biopsy is over. How do you see God working in and around your child's crisis?

Love Notes

Let your friends in crises tell you how they see God working rather than tell them what you see. Words like "Oh, but you're becoming so strong through this!" come across as "I'm so glad it's you and not me."

WHY IS CHARLIE IN A WHEELCHAIR?

"Something went wrong while he was growing inside his mother. While his spine was forming, a place didn't close all the way. Part of his spinal cord stayed exposed, and his legs don't work as a result. It's called spina bifida. He's very smart,

and happy, and friendly. In fact, he's great in math. His legs are the only things about him that don't work. There is more the same about you two than different."

Just as other things go wrong in this world, bodies can go wrong. There's seldom a clear cause—things just happen. It's hard, frustrating, and confusing. But it's reality. Children understand broken things. What they don't understand is why those broken things can't be fixed. Admit that you also wish all broken bodies could be fixed. Look forward to heaven where we'll all have perfect bodies.

An important question lurks behind your child's "why" and "how." He wonders, "Can it happen to me?" Be very honest as you answer: "Your spine has already formed so you can't get spina bifida. But other things could happen that might cause you to be in a wheelchair. I don't expect that to happen; but if it does, I'll be beside you to help you. In the meantime, why don't you say, 'Hello,' to Charlie?"

Both children and adults avoid handicapped peers because they fear catching the handicap. This is not logical or even possible, but we people aren't always logical. Address this fear so your child won't act on it. Show your child how to take steps toward friendship so he can discover the beauty in his handicapped friend. Every person is unique and exciting; handicaps change none of that.

No one is happy when a child is born without sight, struggles to learn, or must maneuver with a wheelchair. But people become happy when they get to know this one-of-a-kind child. People are people whether blind, learning disabled, paralyzed, or otherwise challenged. We can enjoy and cherish each other. Birth defects can't steal the joy of friendship, family, togetherness, accomplishment, or love. We really can overcome evil with good.

Love Notes

NEVER use another person to make you or your child feel better. Words like "Be thankful for your legs because Owen has none," or "There's always someone worse off than you are," imply that other people suffer for your benefit. It's also incredibly cruel and insensitive. Finally, it separates person from person. See people as people, not "the handicapped girl" or the "Down's syndrome boy." Refuse such attitudes as "I'm glad you could have the experience of knowing a retarded person." Instead, promote "We're all equally valuable, we all have something to contribute, and we're all worth knowing."

BUT WHY ARE THERE BIRTH DEFECTS ANYWAY?

"They're part of the imperfect world we live in. Things can go wrong here. We don't like it. God doesn't like it. And one day He will stop it. In the meantime Satan takes what God has given and twists it. As we work with God, we can untwist some of the bad things and find ways to manage the other things. You and Charlie can be good friends, go to each other's birthday parties, and enjoy life. His paralyzed legs can't get in the way of that. Romans 8 explains that this world waits for perfection. We can wait for it. And we can look forward to enjoying perfectly working bodies in heaven.

Your perceptive and sensitive child doesn't want anyone to suffer, not himself or his friend. Agree that birth defects and disabilities from other causes hurt you too. Then list together all the good things the handicap can't stop.

Even when we know the cause of the birth defect, we can't always fix it. In my Sarah's case, something apparently went wrong while her ears were forming. No one knows for certain, but all the known causes for hearing loss have been ruled out. Even if we knew the specific cause, we couldn't fix it. So now we've got to find ways around it.

She uses hearing aids, FM systems, and lip-reading to hear and understand as much as possible. Charlie uses a wheelchair, physical therapy, and the love of his family and friends. One day both Sarah and Charlie will experience perfectly working bodies in heaven. In the meantime, they and we experience happiness in a relationship called faith—God gives security and gets us through. He is the bedrock foundation in life that no problem can break. He provides the friends, abilities, and opportunities to enjoy and participate in life, no matter what the obstacles. His love cannot be diminished no matter what bad thing happens. Herein lies the answer to the fear behind your child's question—can my friend be happy? The answer is most certainly yes.

> Herein lies the answer to the fear behind your child's question—can my friend be happy? The answer is most certainly yes.

"For I am convinced that neither death nor life, neither angels nor demons, neither the present nor the future, nor any powers, neither height nor depth, nor anything else in all creation, will be able to separate us from the love of God that is in Christ Jesus our Lord" (Rom. 8:38-39).

But It's Not Fair!

"You're right. Life on this earth is not fair. Good people suffer horrible things while bad people never seem to have so much as a cold. But even when life is unfair, it can be good— we can always work around the problem to find and make happiness."

We need to affirm the smart things our children say. This child is right—life is not fair. Unfairness is a fact of life on earth. We save ourselves much agony by simply admitting this and then doing our best in spite of it. We can concentrate on the ability to choose joy based in God, no matter what the circumstances. We can look forward to heaven. We can make this world more heaven-like by choosing kind words and loving actions.

Even when we accept it, the unfairness can get to us. This frustration is OK. See chapter 5 for suggestions on walking with your child through these angry feelings. Sometimes it helps to yell about it: "I hate these silly broken cochlea that keep me from hearing well. It's not fair and I don't like it one bit. Yuck! Yuck! Yuck!" We've spent many a car ride home from grueling hearing tests quite noisily protesting Sarah's hearing situation. Exhausted from both test and protest, we end up laughing and feel united as a family. We know we'll make it because God is with us.

We Dockreys find great comfort in the fact that when sad things happen, God suffers just as deeply as we do. He then takes us in His arms and loves us through the sadness. We want to understand the hows and whys as far as is humanly possible. What we don't understand, we entrust to Him. We know that bit-by-bit God is guiding His people back to the perfect happiness He had in mind when

He created our world. And one day we'll be in a place where life is good forever (Rev. 21:4). As the hymn says, "We'll understand it better by and by."

WILL IT HURT?

"Yes, but only for a little while. I'll be right here beside you to hold your hand. And when it's over we'll go to the museum."

Saying, "It won't hurt," is acting like the toddler who covers her eyes and says, "You can't see me." When your child must undergo a painful procedure, tell her what will happen, about how long it will hurt, and how to get through it. Then stay with her and walk through the pain together. We must be honest about pain or our children won't be able to believe us.

"Yes, but…" often works well in answering this question. "Yes, it will hurt; but we'll make it fast," or "Yes, it will be hard, but as soon as it's over, we'll go to the cafeteria." Learn your child's best timing—some like to know about the pain right before they experience it; others need time to get ready. Chapter 2 offers specific techniques and words to use when your child must go through pain.

AM I GOING TO DIE?

"Yes, you will die sometime, but we don't know when. The disease you fight has killed many children. Other children have recovered. We hope you're one of those who lives a long, long life. But if you die young, we know Jesus will take care of you in heaven until we get there. And if we die before you do,

Grandmama and Granddaddy will take care of you here on earth. What do you think death will be like?"

Like many adults, children can't imagine their lives ending. But they wonder when death will happen to them and what it will be like. We can never say, "No, you won't die," because even some children in perfect health die young. If a life-threatening illness doesn't get them, a car accident or another unforeseen tragedy could. Let your answer cover two important fears: (1) What will happen to me when I die? and (2) What will happen to me if you die first?

As Christians we can unequivocally assure our children of life after death. When our children love and accept Jesus, they spend the rest of their lives with Him. As we tell our children that God wants to take care of them forever, we encourage them toward faith and salvation. We feed their natural trust in God.

Children's biggest fear of death is not knowing what will happen. An eleven-year-old explains, "You're used to someone being close by to tell you what will come next. With death your parents can't go with you."

As we assure our children that Jesus will care for them and that we'll be in heaven soon, we ease their fears. In fact, some children prefer dying before their parents—they don't want to be left here alone.

Invite your children to share their ideas about death and dying. They often have even better insight into heaven than we do. Try questions like: "What do you think about dying?" "What do you think heaven will be like?" "Would you rather die first or me die first?" "Will you save a seat for me if you go first?" We don't know exactly what dying or death will be like. But your children's images reveal their hopes and beliefs. In the middle of a long and critical night in the hospital a fifteen-year-old said, "Mom, I don't want you to worry. If I live, it will be a miracle; and if I die, it will be a miracle too because I will live forever."

Talking about death is taboo in our society. We say, "He passed away," or "She went to heaven." Our emotions say, "If I die," rather than "When I die." Push yourself to talk about death so your child won't worry alone. Then celebrate that, though death is terrible, it is not the end.

T.I.P.S. FOR ANSWERING QUESTIONS

Each question your child asks is an opportunity to strengthen his faith actions and life skills. Let these four criteria guide your answers:

True: You can't assure your paralyzed son that he'll walk again if he has enough faith. These holy-sounding words play a cruel joke on your son. Base your hope in God's reality, not on wishful thinking. Make your answers true. This does not mean you communicate gloom and doom. It means you assure your son he can surmount all obstacles and can find ways to get where he wants to go no matter how difficult. You assure him that God will always be with Him, and you'll be there every time it is humanly possible. You assure him that he'll have a perfect body in heaven.

Invite God's Wisdom: Search Scripture, listen to God, and notice how God works in everyday life in order to give answers that God would give. Don't substitute what you wish God would say or what you've heard that God says.

Put Your Answers to Work: When you answer that life is not fair, but we can choose and create happiness anyway, let your child see you doing that. When you answer that troubles are a part of this world but not the only part, let your child see you focus on the good rather than whine about the problems. When you answer that God doesn't like disabilities but works around them to create good, get your child the speech therapy and hearing aids she needs to talk clearly, let your child join teams and lessons with peers, and equip your child to get on with living. Chapters 3, 6, and 7 share some ways to do these things.

Short: Children seldom want a long discourse. Give a sentence or two and then invite your child to share what she thinks about the question and answer. Give and take is the best way to discover answers to your child's questions. See chapter 1 for sample discussions about death and other tough subjects.

Keep it short in another way—refuse to dwell on *why* questions for long. Save your energy for the more important *what now* questions.

Bonus Resources

Books specifically written to walk with teens through grief over death and other painful experiences are *It's Not Fair: Through Grief to Healing* and *Youthcare*. Both are published by New Hope Publishers; the first is for teens and the other is for those who care about teens. A third book, *Facing Down the Tough Stuff* (Chariot), includes young teens' stories about their own grief. Check in your church media library for these books.

LIVE YOUR ANSWERS

Your children will learn most of their answers to tough questions by watching you live. Lisa, a first-grade teacher, tells about a student with a cleft palate. This child's parents were very anxious about how other children would react to their son. Because they feared classmates would reject him, they delayed his starting school for a year and a half. When he finally came to school, children never criticized him or treated him differently. They just wondered why he was so quiet. His parents' protectiveness had kept him from developing the confidence he needed to respond to his classmates' offers of friendship. Lisa recalls, "I never saw one child make fun of his scar or voice. They only commented on his quietness. He had several friends by the end of the year.

> I'm convinced Anna takes her cues for how to respond to her crisis from me.

"I understand the parents' protective instinct," Lisa continues. "My daughter Anna lost all of her hair because of a rare inherited condition called alopecia. I dread meeting new people with my little bald girl. But I have to overcome that for her sake. I see my attitude as the key. If I know and communicate that she can do it, she can do it.

"I'm convinced Anna takes her cues for how to respond to her crisis from me. When her hair was almost gone, I swallowed hard and asked her, 'How would you feel if you lost all your hair?'

" 'How would you feel?' Anna returned the question.

" 'Well, I'd feel a little sad,' I answered.

" 'Me, too. I want to put my hair up like Mary Poppins, but I'd look like Jesse (her bald baby doll),' she said with a giggle."

"When she takes her hat off in church or wherever, I have to stifle hard my urge to cover her head," admits Lisa. "But I remind myself that what matters to me is not what others think, but what Anna thinks."

There's nothing wrong about parental feelings of protectiveness. We simply have to translate those feelings into actions that will truly protect our children—actions like assuring them that they can do it and giving them the skills to do so. Keeping our children away from people won't protect them. Nurturing their natural confidence about the good God has created in them will. Equipping them to face their challenges will. Standing beside them through thick and thin, easy and hard will.

THE POINT ←

God, not smoothly uttered truths about Him, is our answer. Rather than just say He is our answer, we must live it. We lean on God's everlasting arms, heal through His care, act as He instructs, share His wisdom, and tap into His power for going on with life. He is our Advocate, our Equipper, our Source of power, the one Unchangeable Constant in our lives. He is the Giver of good gifts, gifts that persist in the midst of pain. As our Answer, He gives us the specific answers that help us through whatever our children face.

Chapter 9

Expect Family Pain

"Dear friends, do not be surprised at the painful trial you are suffering as though something strange were happening to you....Commit [yourself] to [your] faithful Creator and continue to do good."
—1 Peter 4:12,19

"I want to share with you some of the feelings the sibling of a sick child feels," offered Rita, whose brother suffered repeatedly with complications of diabetes. "Sadness—for despite everyday spats, no child is dearer. Desertion—because Mommy and Daddy don't have much time for the healthy one. Guilt—because the other child is sick, not yourself, and because you can't stop being interested in good things of life. Fear—because all this might happen to you. I felt all these things, buy my main memory emotionally is the joy when my brother survived his first critical illness and came back home to us. The long-term result has been to make him much dearer to me than I think he would have been without the illness."

Trish battled scoliosis throughout childhood and adolescence. Her sister shares, "I viewed what she was going through as temporary, though the casting dragged on for four years. It was a plus that Trish had a great sense of humor and could laugh at herself. The rest of us, deeply saddened at what she went through, tried hard not to show much pity. We just silently admired her courage. She didn't allow herself to cave in and handled the surgeries with mental toughness."

As Randy watched his brother Reid suffer repeated flare-ups from rheumatoid arthritis, he struggled deeply with why. "Why is this happening to my brother?" his mother recalls his asking. "If God knows all things and makes all things, why did He let arthritis enter the world?" Over the years Randy has found more peace with the struggle. But new flare-ups from the arthritis reactivate the questions. Reid, on the other hand, finds the struggles less complicated. He never really fought the *why* question. Maybe in some ways it really is easier to go through suffering than to watch someone you love go through it. His arthritis flares up again and again, yet his joy triumphs. One thing that helps him is when his struggles help someone else bear pain.

Love Notes

When you bring a gift to a child in crisis, bring a little something for siblings too.

RECOGNIZE SIBLING PAIN

Sisters, brothers, mothers, and fathers hurt when a child in the family suffers. This suffering comes in many packages—questions, jealousy, anger, depression, confusion, strife, intensity, clinging, irritability, school or work problems, and behavior changes. Recognize these as pain. Then guide your family members to interpret and manage it. Children often feel these feelings without being able to put them into words. As we recognize and respond to this suffering, we make it as a family.

"It's not fair that you and Emily get to go to the hospital and I have to go to school! You'll get to go to the cafeteria and play games and all that fun stuff. I won't," lamented Sarah.

No matter how frequently Emily explains that the shots, spinals, and bone marrow biopsies just aren't worth the fun, Sarah sees our monthly cancer clinic visits as not-to-be-missed adventures. She wants to be involved. So we take her along when she's not in school, and we fill her in on everything that happens when she can't go. If Emily goes out for lunch or dessert, she brings something back for Sarah. When Emily opens her after-clinic surprise, we provide one for Sarah. Because Sarah worries about Emily as well as wants to go along, we let Sarah's teacher know the days of Emily's clinic visits so she can give Sarah a little extra tender loving care that day. These tiny bits of effort keep Sarah from feeling abandoned, heal her fears, and make her feel a part of our very important cancer fight. They also keep Emily's compassion alive and growing. Even when she's the primary focus, Emily looks beyond her pain to care for her sister.

Siblings of children in crisis need their parents just as much as the more obviously hurting one. Provide hugs, a listening ear, and plentiful paper for writing and drawing. Then at the earliest possible opportunity, provide your presence.

While Ingrid spent six weeks in the hospital with Chad for a bone marrow transplant, there was no way she could give presence to her other two children. She could not leave Chad's hospital room because of the risk of picking up a virus and bringing it back to Chad. So she gave herself through phone calls, window visits, and Grandma. Her mother came to stay with the two siblings and give the mama-love Ingrid was unable to give. Dane, Ingrid's husband, helped by reading stories, listening to adventures and misadventures, and reporting every detail of the hospital experience. Ingrid had left a package of special surprises for each day she was gone. The children opened one gift a day to help the days without Mama pass by more quickly. Counting the remaining gifts helped them know just how long they had to wait.

When Ingrid and Chad returned home, things did not automatically return to normal. Eighteen-month-old Curtis clung to his daddy, unconvinced that Ingrid was really home to stay. Four-year-old Cara bickered jealously with Chad, unconsciously angry with him for taking Mama away for so long. As Ingrid and Dane gradually resumed their usual roles, all five family members felt more at home and happy. As Ingrid and Dane assured each other that they would make it through this rough time, they felt empowered to meet the needs of their three children. Expecting a measure of upheaval makes it a bit easier to cope with.

Child's Viewpoint

Siblings of children in crisis feel the intensity of the crisis without always understanding what they feel or why. Heal their lonely fear by listening to what they have to say. Explain what is happening and ask them how they feel about it. Refuse to try to protect them from hurt—it's impossible. Siblings sense our feelings and the feelings of the child in crisis. The only way to ease sibling hurt is to help them make sense of the feelings. Clearly explain what is happening and what they can do about it:

"Chad is in the hospital to heal him of his cancer. You remember when he had lots of medicine called chemotherapy? It was not strong enough and the cancer came back. So now he has to get even stronger treatment and then some new bone marrow. He'll get some of Cara's bone marrow and Cara will grow some more. The strong treatments make it easy for him to get sick, so he has to stay in a room where there are no germs. Soon he'll be able to fight off germs, and then he can come home. While Mama and Chad are in the hospital, you can help Grandma and Daddy and you can make cards for Chad."

What children imagine is always worse than the truth. Don't let them suffer alone. Tell them what's happening and what it means.

CHERISH YOUR SPOUSE

We parents feel the pain of both the child in crisis and her siblings. Walking together makes it easier to meet the needs of our children. One of the greatest pleasures I share with my husband, Bill, is sitting in the same room together at the end of the day. We don't always talk or even do the same thing—we just "be." This homey and happy togetherness gives me stability and strength to meet the next day's challenges. I've discovered that cherishing this closeness is as important as "doing" something about our marriage. Much marriage advice emphasizes going out together, talking things over, learning new things about each other. I agree that these are important, but times of crisis leave little energy or money for romantic candlelight encounters and all-night talks. So we learn about each other and grow close by simply sharing the good and bad of life, by talking about how to handle the day-to-day hurdles each member of our family faces. The pressure to go out would add one more demand to our already unmeetable demand list. So rather than ask one more thing from each other, we cherish each other—a few minutes at the end of every day to give each other the freedom to be, and to be loved.

I'm convinced that pure exhaustion is one reason marriages break up when a child suffers. There's just no emotional energy left to keep the marriage strong. Bill and I realize how low our energy is, so we try to spend it carefully. We restrain irritating words and caustic comments. We expect minor annoyances to feel like monumental emergencies, so we purposely disregard them. We deliberately replace exasperation with words of appreciation. This keeps the trivial from invading the precious few moments we share as a couple and family. We don't always succeed at these actions, but life goes more smoothly when we do.

One thing Bill has taught me so well is the power of acceptance. He loves me as I am rather than demand that I change. His blanket of acceptance gives me the security to whittle off my rough edges and treat him with the same kindness he gives me. When we truly accept each other, each of us finds motivation to give our best to the other. When Bill works long hours, I remember that his dedication is precisely what attracted me to him

I'm convinced that pure exhaustion is one reason marriages break up when a child suffers. There's just no emotional energy left to keep the marriage strong.

in the first place. He gives the girls and me the same unswerving loyalty he gives to his job. That's a given. We can count on it. Cherishing his loyalty is so much better than bickering about his work habits.

Acceptance has also given us ammunition to battle our children's crises. We can't change the hearing loss, so we find ways around it. We can't wish away the cancer, so we fight it with medicine and hope. The disability and disease don't alter our love—they simply mean we rally as a family to conquer each challenge.

Herein lies the second reason marriages get into trouble when a child suffers: one or both parents refuse to accept the disability, disease, or change. They say, "I can't handle it." What they really mean is "I refuse to help." Nobody likes crises and nobody chooses them. If protesting would make crises vanish, we'd all do it. But it won't. A parent who turns away from his child's crisis doubles the difficulty—his child then has not only the crisis but also an absent parent to grieve. Much better is to band together and fight the evil as a family.

Sadly, one parent can't make this choice for another. A parent who chooses to whine, fuss, and attack his family is seldom open to learning from the other. After Willie's son was diagnosed with learning disabilities, she unintentionally developed a habit of criticizing him: "You give me so much trouble! Every time we get one problem solved, I have to traipse back up to the school." She also complained to her husband, "He can't do anything by himself!" How much happier Willie, her son, and her husband would be if Willie had cherished her son, had chosen to act on the truth that he is worth the work it takes to equip him to succeed in school, and then had empowered him with skills and encouragement.

Every family has problems. Every parent wishes things were at least a little different. Everyone gets irritated during physical or emotional pain. Everybody needs extra loving during hard times. We choose what to do about this dilemma—we either move past our pain to care for others, or we stay focused on ourselves and multiply the pain for ourselves and our family. We choose to embrace the good or nurture our misery. We decide to create joy or feel sorry for ourselves. We choose to cherish family closeness whatever the circumstance, or we waste precious family happiness by taking our frustrations out on each other.

Marissa, a teenager who witnessed the repeated pain of her Sunday School teacher's child, wrote this letter: "You five have been through so much, but I still sense such a joy in you. It appears to come from your love for each other. It's obvious that your family enjoys being together. You and your wife really seem to like each other, and your family has such great times. I admire you."

That's the kind of family I want to have.

TO MAKE IT THROUGH A LONG-TERM CRISIS

Gail Linam, parent of a now grown daughter who was diagnosed with juvenile rheumatoid arthritis at age eight, suggests this advice to families in continuing crises:

(1) First, I take enormous comfort and courage from the fact that I wasn't and still am not in it alone, that God is walking with me through it. I found and find it profoundly comforting that the God who created all things walks with me. If His power can make a whole world, He has the strength to help me.

(2) Second, taking life one day at a time is very liberating. It's impossible for any of us to know the whole story and all that the future holds. We can't do everything that needs doing in this one day. This day and this hour are enough. With God's help I will make it through this hour. Of course we have to plan and prepare to provide for future days, but we must give ourselves permission to let some things go undone, to not accomplish or know the whole plan at once.

(3) Third, link up to a support structure that offers more than opinions. Find a group, a newsletter, a person that

offers accurate and up-to-date information about your child's crisis. We ordered a newsletter on juvenile rheumatoid arthritis. Our pediatrician and his team became our support group. Without a network, you can't possibly stay abreast of everything. With one, you know you're doing everything you can. Even when answers aren't complete, you can forge ahead with confidence.

(4) Closely related to number 3 is to open yourself to a few friends you trust. Join a prayer group or Bible study group that does not have your child's disease as its exclusive focus. This coming together for spiritual support and Bible study gives each member opportunity to weep with and celebrate with the others. Without a group like this, the tunnel vision of our own suffering keeps us from the whole picture of life.

(5) Finally, make a pledge to keep on growing as a person. To respond to your child's needs and urge her on to life at its fullest, you need to grow, too. Take mental journeys through books and tapes and explore the ways you can keep your mind active and searching. Learn from people. Live the spiritual truths you discover.

SHARE THE PAIN WITH YOUR EXTENDED FAMILY

Grandparents, aunts, uncles, and cousins will also hurt when crises come to your child. Eric telephoned his father and brother with the sobering news that his newborn son had Down's syndrome. Both assured Eric of their love and support. They said they looked forward to meeting the newest member of the family. Sounding calm and collected, they expressed their love for Eric and his wife.

Later, Eric's brother David pulled Eric aside and said, "I know he wouldn't tell you himself, but Dad cried when he heard the diagnosis."

That same day, Eric's dad privately said, "I know he wouldn't tell you himself, but David cried when he heard the diagnosis."

Why do we family members hesitate to tell each other when we feel sad? Perhaps we believe we must be strong for each other. Perhaps we consider tears a sign of hopelessness. Maybe we fear that sadness indicates lack of trust in God. In reality, strength comes from sharing pain, not from feeling it alone. The Bible encourages us to "weep with those who weep" (Rom. 12:15 GNB).

Certainly there are times we must push aside our fears to go on with the medical procedure; times we must squelch our worries to rejoice with someone who's feeling optimistic; times we hush to listen to another. But most often, mutual talking disperses the power of fear. Crying together makes us feel loved. Writing letters about worries helps us see the solid future we really have. Let's free ourselves to weep together, to share the pain, to lift each other up by being down together.

As we extended family members care for each other, we refresh and equip each other for the pivotal role of caring for our children in crises. We empower each other to stay up all night, to remain patient during the grueling procedures, to steadily meet the daily challenges of a continuing disability.

My in-laws are especially good at this consistent care. They call following each hearing recheck and each chemo visit to find out just what happened and just what is coming. They feel disappointed along with us when Sarah's hearing drops and rejoice with us when it comes back up even slightly. They visit Emily during her chemo weeks to distract her from the pain. They learn about Sarah's latest speech challenge and guide her to master it. They show interest in other areas of the girls' lives. They give specific help. They motivate all four of us to work toward a happy future without assuming that journey toward happiness will be easy. They hug us and listen as we share our pain. They share their hopes, fears, and dreams with us.

SURVIVE THE NOT-SO-CARING

Not all relatives are this helpful. Nadia assumes that if she claps loudly enough and believes hard enough, all the problems will go away. Rather than help young Sonny with his hearing crisis, she just talks. In every letter she says, "I hope Sonny's hearing is better and everything is fine now." She refuses to accept that Sonny's hearing loss is permanent or that it impacts Sonny in any way. When Sonny was first diagnosed, she said, "They'll come up with a cure." Every time she sees Sonny, she says, "Everybody has trouble hearing sometimes. I don't see that much difference in him."

Nadia's eyes avoid Sonny's hearing aids. She has no idea how to work them, and she asks Sonny to take them out for family pictures, which Sonny wisely refuses to do. She gives no practical help such as reinforcing speech lessons, turning down the radio so Sonny can hear the conversation, or facing Sonny so he can understand what she's saying. Nadia pretends everything is OK. Her unwillingness to accept the reality of the challenge, the helpfulness of hearing strategies, and the pain of the journey creates a tension that is confusing to Sonny and painful to Sonny's parents.

Stephen's legs were paralyzed in a diving accident. His uncle puts him on a pedestal with words like "Stephen, you're so brave and wonderful." Stephen wishes his uncle would just treat him normally. Stephen knows he's not a hero—he's just a regular kid with legs that don't work. It really gets to him when his uncle brings God into it by saying, "This will be such a testimony." Stephen believes that a testimony is obeying God in everyday life, not having a bad experience. If he had listened to God and refused the daredevil dive, he wouldn't be in the wheelchair in the first place. Stephen and God have made peace with what happened. Stephen knows he can't change the past and refuses to dwell on it. He wishes everyone else would do that, too. He wants his paralyzed legs to be just a part of his life, not all of it. Stephen wants people to ask about other parts of his life like school, friends, and church. God helps with those, too. Why can't his uncle understand this?

Teresa's five-year-old daughter lost a kidney to a Wilms' tumor. When she shared her concern with her cousin Cathy, Cathy dispensed a profusion of Bible verses and certain-to-work wisdom. She told Teresa, "Your worry shows you don't have enough faith. If you truly had faith, you would be able to stop worrying." After Cathy questioned the quality of Teresa's faith, Teresa had not only her daughter to worry about but also her faith. Teresa felt severed from the very people she had formerly turned to for help. She wanted to explain that her worry was a sign of caring, not the absence of faith. She wanted to remind

Cathy that, when Jesus cried over Lazarus, observers recognized it as love. She wanted to say that she did trust God and that talking to relatives helped her live this trust. But she said nothing. She felt unable to confide her deepest thoughts and concerns with her family, because she no longer had the security that they would give her the care she so acutely needed.

If your relatives add to your pain rather than ease it, drain your enthusiasm rather than refresh it, you may have to limit your time with them. Rather than try to change or cater to your less-than-helpful relative, save your limited energy to care for your child. Work toward that delicate balance between understanding and shielding your family from extra hurt.

Nobody means to hurt. They're as sad as you are about the crisis. They want to make it better, to take away the pain. So they give an answer. They don't realize that easy answers make things worse instead of better. They don't know that quoting holy-sounding words comes across as a put-down to your faith. They really are trying to help. But it still hurts.

"I try to just let the insensitive comments and actions roll off my back and focus on the wonderfully appropriate things people say and do," Lynda explains. "I do open mail to my chronically ill child, especially if I don't know who it is from. I'm afraid someone might tell him that if he'd just do this, he'd be healed; that this crisis is a wonderful gift; or some other blasphemy. Rather than wasting worry on what people do or don't do, I give my energy to caring for my child."

Love Notes

Become an even more caring relative with ideas like these:

If you tend toward this	*Do this instead*
Don't worry; everything will be fine: Have you refused to listen to or accept your family member's pain, assumed it would go away, or casually proclaimed that God will take care of it?	**Ask questions**: Your family member is hungry for someone who will listen to and remember details. Ask: "What did the doctor say? What is the next step? How do you feel about it?" Don't try to fix or interpret or "blessing-ize." Simply show genuine interest.
It's not that bad: Do you pretend the crippled legs will start growing correctly any day? Do you dismiss worry with, "They'll come up with a cure by the time he's a teenager," or "Nobody dies from that anymore?" Have you assumed that kids can handle things better than adults?	**Feel the pain**: It's sad and hard when a child gets sick, copes with a disability, or is injured. Go ahead and feel the pain and let your family member know you care. When Jesus wept, people recognized it as a sign of love (John 11:35-36). One reason we resist pain is we can hardly bear it to happen to someone we love. Go ahead and say you wish it hadn't happened; don't pretend it didn't.

Love Notes

Become an even more caring relative with ideas like these:

If you tend toward this	*Do this instead*
I just can't face it: Have you abandoned the child in crisis by claiming you can't handle it? Do you put off learning about the wheelchair, how to help cope with side effects, how to do the therapy, and other actions that would specifically help the child and his family?	**Learn how to face it**: Ask how to help your retarded cousin learn, how to thump the back of your niece with cystic fibrosis, how to work the wheelchair, how to make side effects easier. Choose to help solve the pain rather than avoid it. The child and his family need you.
You're so brave: Do you put the child on a pedestal, making him a hero, and effectively isolating him? Do you distance yourself from the child by saying things about him rather than go through the hard things with him? Have you seen bravery or do you just say it because it sounds nice?	**Go through tough times with the child**: Go along for a doctor visit and ask how you can help. When your child manages a vision test with concentration or takes a shot without screaming, do express your pride. But expand your pride to schoolwork, friendship, and other non-crisis skills.

GET THROUGH EACH EPISODE OF PAIN

"Mommy, my ear hurts," said Penny's pajama-clad toddler at her bedside. She glanced at the clock: 3:30 A.M. As she picked Ted up and began to rock him, Penny lamented, "Not another ear infection—we just finished the antibiotic last week!" She vacillated between calling the doctor immediately in hopes that an antibiotic would keep his eardrum from rupturing or waiting until morning in case the infection might be too new to diagnose correctly. She recalled times she'd gone in immediately, only to have the noticeable signs of infection develop an hour after returning home.

Penny rocked her son until he fell asleep in the chair. Sitting up eased the pressure in his ear, and he was able to rest. While Penny rocked, that too-familiar pain seeped through her. For several days Ted would struggle to hear over the muffling effect of ear fluid. His hearing aids would be useless. Each infection brought to the forefront the fact that no doctor on the face of the earth could solve the continuing infections or repair Ted's hearing.

Penny knew that pain in Ted's ears meant an almost certain ear infection; the only question was how far along it was. That little "almost" kept her from confident decision. She had starter doses of antibiotic that the doctor had given her for future infections. She also knew that starting the antibiotic might confuse a diagnosis later in the day. She decided to wait until 7:00 A.M. She realized there were no definite answers, but she wanted an answer so badly. She reasoned that morning was early enough to get her son started on antibiotic, but late enough to make sure what kind of infection was starting.

By morning Penny noticed pus draining from Ted's ear. His eardrum had burst. Should she have started the antibiotic or called the doctor when he first complained? Or was it already too late when Ted felt the pressure? Penny relived the scene a hundred times. In the revised version she took Ted on to the doctor, and they caught the infection just before it burst the eardrum.

Telling Penny not to worry about Ted's burst eardrum is futile. But the way she worries is the key. Simply fretting won't help. Neither will refusing to think about it. But reviewing the past to decide what to do next time will help. Penny decided to talk with the doctor about her course of action to see how to modify it next time. She reasoned that it may be better to start the antibiotic at the first sign of ear pain just in case it would stop the fluid buildup. She becomes comfortable with the past as she goes back over memories and makes decisions for the future.

Family pain comes most often in a series of relatively minor challenges, not as huge life-or-death events. As any parent knows, these challenges don't feel so minor when they involve our children, and in many ways they're not minor at all. A series of ear infections can hinder speech development. A critical peer can undermine confidence in ways that take years to repair. Each crisis is a crucial one.

Life is hard and we just have to do the best we can. Philip Yancey explains in his book, *In His Image:*

"The pictorial Chinese language combines the two concepts of love and pain in eloquent symbolism. In the character that expresses the highest kind of love, symbols for love and pain are brushed on top of each other to form a word like 'pain-love'. Thus a mother 'pain-loves' her child. She pours out her whole being on the child's behalf."

This is how we love our children, whether in crisis or in calm. This is how God loves us. We "pain-love" our children with energy and inventiveness and then ride out the crises to the calm between the storms.

CHERISH THE CALM BETWEEN STORMS

Penny makes the most of times Ted is free of ear infections, talking with him often to make up for the times his hearing is muffled. She consults specialists to discover whether the ear tubes that haven't helped before might help this time. She remains alert to new medications and treatments, hoping someone will offer treatment that will whip Ted's persistent problem.

I too have learned the importance of treasuring routine days and normal happenings. It was months after our daughter's cancer diagnosis before I really felt like working again. But each day I made myself sit at my desk and do something. Surprisingly, just that little bit of success made me feel that the day was worthwhile. I was still able to produce something significant, even though I hurt so badly. Work reminded me that good really could come in the middle of crises. Emily really could continue with school, with learning, with growing. One of my most distressing fears had been that cancer would halt Emily's growth—experientially, emotionally, intellectually, spiritually. But daily routine reminded me that life can and will go on, and that the life that goes on is a good one.

Walking with Emily through chemo offers us three weeks of relative calm followed by an absolutely excruciating week. This fourth week begins with nervous fear about the pain to come, an extended day of chemotherapy and check-ups, and six days of steadily worsening side effects. During this week we feel we'll never see the light of day—Emily's discomfort just gets worse and worse. Her sleepless nights get longer and longer. We try to remember that there's an end. We've seen it before, so it has to come again. Just four more days...just three more days...this is the worst day...now the second worst...now just one last day. Ahhh, how wonderful that you can feel good again, Emily.

We just have to ride these painful days as best we can, keeping our eyes on the hope at the end. We ask God to guide us to respond through each intense wave of pain with love and grace. We ask for actions that will distract Emily from the agony. God walks right beside us, holding us up physically and emotionally.

Then those lovely days of relative calm come. And I'm tempted to complain when the light bulb burns out or the mail is late. I'm learning to squelch unnecessary fussing to cherish these moments of calm. For some crises, the good times are as brief as minutes or hours, but they are equally important to cherish. Especially if your crisis is a continuing one, don't wait to enjoy life. Find joy between the ear infections, the arthritic flare-ups, the physical obstacles. Life is too short to waste even a moment.

Bonus Resources

Other parents who have suffered along with a child can offer you the tools you need to make it through your pain. John Claypool offers valuable insight in his poignant book *Tracks of a Fellow Struggler* (Word Publishing, 1974). His ten-year-old daughter died after a battle with leukemia.

LET HOPE CARRY YOU THROUGH

The good news is that family pain is not the end of the story. There are better days coming and there are better days now. We can make it because God is real and because He has promised to bring us through the pain to pain-free days. Step by step we can meet the challenges of that day. Ultimately, there will be an end to the suffering, either here or in heaven. This hope is certain, real, and dependable: "And hope does not disappoint us, because God has poured out his love into our hearts by the Holy Spirit, whom he has given us" (Rom. 5:5).

While God's people were in exile, God gave them words of hope. The same promises hold for us today. We and our children will make it because of God:

" 'You will call upon me and come and pray to me, and I will listen to you. You will seek me and find me when you seek me with all your heart. I will be found by you,' declares the Lord, 'and will bring you back from captivity' " (Jer. 29:12-14).

SEE PAIN AS A PART OF LIFE

So what do we do with the complex pain that washes over not only a child in crisis but also her siblings, uncles, cousins, aunts, and grandparents? First, we expect it, not in a gloomy or fatalistic way, but as a part of life. Because we are caring and loving people, we will hurt when things go wrong. It's OK to say that you, your child, and your family feel hurt, tired, and overwhelmed. While battling their son's cancer, one family explained, "We're in anticipatory, retroactive, and present grief. We grieve for the future wondering if the cancer will return. We grieve looking back over what has already happened. And we grieve because of the present pain caused by the chemotherapy." It's no challenge to faith to say you feel very shaken. You know your foundation in God is steady, just like the house upon the rock: "The rain came down, the streams rose, and the winds blew and beat against that house; yet it did not fall, because it had its foundation on the rock" (Matt. 7:25).

Second, when pain comes, keep on living. Move on through it and do good in spite of it (1 Pet. 4:12,19). Embrace the joy while not forgetting about the pain. Rita enjoyed her brother each time they played together. Trish and her sister focused their energies on making genuine and lasting friendships.

During crises you won't feel great, nor should you. You will ache, not celebrate. This doesn't mean you're faithless. It means you're in touch with reality.

Randy tried to do well in school even when his brother was excused from homework during a flare-up. Refuse to look back at what might have been or wait to see what the future will bring. If we spend our lives regretting or waiting, we will miss the good that is present right now. We must look back long enough to heal and look ahead long enough to plan, but not long enough to miss present opportunities for joy.

Third, recognize how faith and pain fit together. Faith is not the same as good feelings. During crises you won't feel great, nor should you. You will ache, not celebrate. This doesn't mean you're faithless. It means you're in touch with reality. Faith is not a sunshiny or happy feeling. It is confidence that God is your solid foundation who holds you up during both terrible and terrific times. Trusting God does not mean denying our emotions; it means listening to His instructions for what to do about them. Sometimes, the only path back to joy is through the pain.

Finally, put your family first and do all you can to build kindness, unity, closeness, and joy. This may mean scaling back on church and community commitments. Rather than feel guilty about this, affirm the family as God's first institution created for love, support, character development, and spiritual teaching (Deut. 6:7). Create the kind of home that walks through pain rather than wallows in it, equips to face challenges rather than worries about them, cherishes people rather than attacks them, and focuses on joy rather than frets about pain.

THE POINT ←

Dealing with long-term crises is just plain rough on the family. Knowing this fact rallies us to cope with it and to keep our families strong. Ration your energy carefully, giving it proportionally to your child in crisis, to your other children, to your marriage, to your work. Fit church service in around these other commitments. Then continue to do good for God's sake, for your family's sake, for your child's sake.

Chapter 10

Choose to Live the Joy

"Tears may linger at nightfall, but joy comes in the morning."
Psalm 30:5 NEB

A single thread has woven through this entire book: We don't have to let the evil steal our joy. There's nothing good about crises like heart problems, cancer, muscular dystrophy, accidents, hearing loss, paralysis, mental impairment—they're insults to the beautifully working bodies God creates. They are never His perfect will. As God agonizes along with us, He supplies joy, a joy that brings hope in the middle of lifelong struggle, skill in the middle of disability, laughter in the middle of pain. These are God's good and perfect gifts. God's joy preempts the present pain and one day will give total triumph. God refuses to let pain have the last word. As the Bible promises, pain will end:

"And God shall wipe away all tears from their eyes; and there shall be no more death, neither sorrow, nor crying, neither shall there be any more pain: for the former things are passed away" (Rev. 21:4).

We can hate the pain for what it is—a distortion of God's beauty—and then move past it to find the good. Leaf back through the chapter titles of this book to find actions that help us do exactly that. Then create a close and loving family with **H.A.P.P.Y.** attitudes like these:

H appiness is a choice.
A ccept pain as sad.
P repare.
P ersist in bringing out good.
Y our children teach you.

H.appiness is a choice: Make the choice to become happy and whole and to pass on this life-foundation to your children: they can choose happiness because of God, not because of what happens or doesn't happen to them. Finding joy is exactly that, a choice. We must choose to discover and enjoy it. When crises come, we can find joy or we can gripe about the bad. There is plenty of both. We simply choose which we'll spotlight. We can live a life we'd be proud to look back on—a life of celebration, joy, love, and togetherness. Or we can whine, complain, envy, and otherwise waste our lives. Crises are not something we can avoid—they're an unhappy fact of life. Move through them rather than bog down in them. Let them be interruptions, not the end of life.

A.ccept pain as sad: We Christians have tremendous trouble with pain. We just don't know where to fit it. Two things are certain: (1) Pain is not the opposite of faith (see the last half of chapter 5); and (2) crises are not good. When a child is born with cerebral palsy, a non-Christian will say, "This is a terrible thing to have happened!" Christians seem compelled to say, "God will bring a blessing out of this." We must go ahead and admit that this is wrong. We must accept that bad things happen in this world and that it's godly to be deeply sad about them. Refuse to "blessing-ize" bad things. Instead call bad "bad," and good "good." Then be sad about the bad, and happy about the good. Don't confuse the two. As Ecclesiastes 3:4 explains: "There is a time to weep and a time to laugh, a time to mourn and a time to dance." Every time pain comes, feel it for what it is. We don't stop at sadness, but we take time to be sad before moving on to be happy.

> Build a relationship with God that is so reliable you can stake your life on it—because you'll have to.

P.repare: Don't wait for crises to grow your faith. During crises you're too tired, too spent, for growing. It's then that you need to lean on everything you've built. Build a relationship with God that is so reliable you can stake your life on it—because you'll have to. Illnesses, accidents, handicaps, problems, and death will plunge our children and families into life-wrenching anguish. God and only God can give us the foundation to make it through such difficult times.

Work at your faith when the going is good. Learn from God's Word daily. Discover God's provision in the everyday miracles like the smiles of your children and the sun that comes up daily without fail. Serve through your church and notice why service is worth making time for.

P.ersist in bringing out good: Crises wear on every member of the family, making tempers short and bickering strong. Muster every scrap of your remaining energy to show kindness to yourself and to motivate your children to be kind. Guide them to respond with grace and compassion, to show Christlikeness. Refuse to make excuses for selfish behavior with words like "He already has so much to deal with that we'll go easy this time." Christlike love is not something we do when we feel like it. It's something we do to make us feel like it.

Love in action is what makes the rough times bearable and the easy times better. Cooperation, encouraging words, honesty, and understanding are the glue that hold our lives together. They are tough to give when we feel drained or sad, but they are the only actions that work.

As a parent, you must be the one who guides your children to love as Jesus loves. No matter how tired you are, give praise for kindness and punishment for cruelty. Provide the consequences that prompt your children to choose thoughtfulness until they are motivated on their own. Grow loving habits through showing them yourself and through insisting that your children do so. Don't let the crises be your excuse for spoiling your children.

Y.our children teach you: As you guide your children through painful times, learn from your children. Following the initial diagnosis of Alicia's hearing loss, her mother would weep with despair and lament, "She's only a hearing aid away from deafness. Will she hear her own babies laugh? How will she manage school and a job? Will anyone look past her poor hearing to see the good in her?" Then Alicia would waken from her nap full of smiles and cuddles. She would play with such joy and intensity that her mother couldn't help but laugh at herself. Alicia knew how to grasp the joy. She taught her mother. When Alicia was nearby, her mother couldn't help but know everything would be fine. Alicia's joy has persisted to this day. With that and a ton of practice, Alicia has done beautifully.

The children who come regularly to the pediatric cancer clinic walk creatively through their continuing crises. While waiting for doctor's appointments, chemotherapy treatments, or drip poles to empty, they pig out on pizza, visit the cafeteria, or hide in their secret meeting room. When one is called to see the doctor, a partner often accompanies her. Anna, close in size to Emily, tries to fool the rookie doctors (residents and fellows) by sitting on Emily's exam table and pretending to be Emily. As one child leaves for the treatment room, the others call out a joke or a tip like, "Cross your legs and wiggle your toes to make the spinal hurt less!" This crowd, at different stages of treatment for a variety of cancers, has let their common challenge form an uncommon bond. They call themselves the clinic gang, and together with God they've created something good to anticipate, something besides shots, spinals, bone marrow biopsies, and IV drips.

> Christlike love is not something we do when we feel like it. It's something we do to make us feel like it.

Appreciate your child's natural wisdom, spontaneous love, and present focus. Then embrace all that is good about childhood, as Jesus encourages: "I tell you the truth, unless you change and become like little children, you will never enter the kingdom of heaven" (Matt. 18:3).

Bonus Resources

One way to grasp joy is to care for other families in pain. Consider joining a group from whom you can receive support as well as give it. Compassionate Friends, P.O. Box 3696, Oak Brook, IL 60522-3696, www.compassionate-friends.org is a nationwide support group for those who mourn the death of a child or sibling. The American Cancer Society, American Diabetes Association, Alexander Graham Bell Association (for deaf and hard of hearing), Arthritis Foundation, Association for Retarded Citizens, Cystic Fibrosis Foundation, Epilepsy Foundation, Leukemia Society, Lupus Foundation of America, and many other specific-to-the-crisis associations provide support groups both locally and nationwide. Check your phone book, search the Internet, and ask your health care givers for current addresses and phone numbers.

CELEBRATE SUPPORT

God sends joy through friends and family who care in specific and helpful ways. One parent tells of two unique gifts her daughter received during a six-week hospitalization. The first was labeled: "INSTANT PARTY: Open when you feel like celebrating."

Inside, the child found party horns, cupcakes, candles, napkins, wrapped favors, and ideas for games that could be played in a hospital room. When it arrived she was too weak to use it. As soon as she was able, she invited everyone on the hall to a party. Could the gift have hurried her recovery?

The second gift was a two-inch box covered with beautiful cloth and lace. The giver said, "This box is for you to keep your memories. Any time you can't bear the pain, open this box and pull out a favorite memory. Your wonderful memories will help you through the hard time."

On the second day of Emily's initial hospitalization, when she felt "like a knife is cutting into my chest," I received a bundle of cards from my youth group. They were full of messages like "You've meant so much to me," and "You've

> As you seek to find and live God's joy, cherish those genuine caregivers who love you in just the way you need it.

helped me understand that God really cares." I was uplifted, encouraged, empowered by the love of these caring youth and the adult who guided them to write.

One dear friend, who knew Emily only by name, became a secret pal to her. She sent her a card every few weeks, sometimes with a surprise inside. Finally she revealed her identity and Emily had a new friend.

Like Emily's secret pal, the most helpful friends are those who continue caring throughout continuing crises. They remember you long past the initial diagnosis. Sarah's speech teacher gives wonderfully encouraging words, like, "You have always treated Sarah as someone who could hear everything. I think you'll continue to do that even with this latest hearing drop. She'll do well." Both her superior teaching skill and her genuine friendship are precious gifts.

Diane put Emily's chemo dates on her calendar and does something special each time. Amazingly, each gift is new and different—once she delivered a package of bubble baths in a variety of shapes and scents. Another time she sent a rose from the florist "since Emily is now grown up enough to enjoy flowers." One month she came by and took Emily to the ice cream store. Still another time she left treats in the back door. Her packaging, delivery method, and gifts are always new and surprising. Best of all, she wraps them in genuine care.

These friends didn't try to ignore or explain away the pain—they brought love in the midst of it. As you seek to find and live God's joy, cherish those genuine caregivers who love you in just the way you need it. Then learn from them and return that care to others.

Some of God's people gifts are not easy to open. When doctors at the hospital presented us with the news that Emily had leukemia, we were anything but pleased. One doctor in particular riled me by asking why I worried so much and by assuring me she wouldn't need to miss much school. Two days earlier he had urged me to allow Emily to run in a distance race, understanding that she might have leukemia. How could he take her life so lightly? I now recognize his casual attitude as a push toward normalcy. He was not convinced that Emily would die, and wanted me to stay equally hopeful. As he encouraged me to let Emily keep doing everything she wanted to do, we escaped saddling her with a sick child image. I assumed that two years of chemotherapy meant missing two years of childhood. He assumed that Emily could fit the chemotherapy around her regular schedule. His enraging calmness prodded me to make sure Emily stayed involved in the very life I feared she would lose. He taught me the value of going on when life is tough. I appreciate him deeply now and Emily adores him. I wasn't so sure then.

Some people aren't gifts from God at all. They are descendants of Job's comforters, eager to tell us exactly the answer to our child's problem, anxious to simplify suffering, quick to advise before they even know the circumstances. Such friends have no time for listening or understanding. Such professionals rudely assume their time is more valuable than yours is. Limit your contact with these. Instead seek family members, friends, and professionals who value both your child and you.

Spend plentiful time with family and friends who see your child as a unique and wonderful person, not "the kid with cancer" or "the second-grader without a leg." Each person has unlimited potential and unlimited chance for fulfillment if allowed—find others who already believe this and promote it yourself. Focus on your child's checker-playing and compassion, rather than her limited mobility. With friends to help you, live as though the crisis is one factor in your child's life, not the main one.

God has promised, "I will not leave you comfortless: I will come to you" (John 14:18 KJV). Celebrate the comfort He provides in the faces of friends, the arms of family members, and the skill of caring doctors and nurses.

Love Notes

Be a joy promoter by being a friend or family member who lives the Bible rather than quotes it. Live Romans 8:28 by bringing good in the midst of the pain. Live Romans 12:15 by listening and crying along with your friend, rather than trying to make it all better. Live Romans 8:38-39 by refusing to desert your friend during rough times. Put aside your hesitation and express God's complete love, the kind that casts out fear and that lays down your life for your friend (1 John 4:18; 3:16). Be a source of joy rather than salt in a wound. Be a doer of the Word, rather than a quoter of the Word (James 1:22). Live the Living Word.

CHERISH LIFE AND HOPE

God, family, and friends will remind you again and again that life is worth living. God is your advocate in your struggle to choose life in the midst of crisis. He weeps with you, rejoices with you, and stays with you. He empowers you and enables you to respond to crisis feelings, to walk with your child through crisis events, and to equip your child to participate fully in life. He guides you as you invite friends to help, move through anger, preserve all that is good about childhood, work with the school, answer questions, make it through the pain, and seize the joy. He is the one Unchanging Constant in your life and in your child's life. He will help you move through the imperfections of this world as you look forward to a time when the pain and imperfection will cease.

God wants to bring good through your child, no matter what the crisis. Through you, He'll give your child loving words, steady discipline, adventuresome days. In your child He'll nurture competence, confidence, and determination to find and cherish what is good in life. Competent (able to) and confident (believing they are able to) children bring joy to people and glory to God. Savor the privilege of working together with God to bring out the good in and to share life with your child.

> God is your advocate in your struggle to choose life in the midst of crisis. He weeps with you, rejoices with you, and stays with you.

- Because your child has been through crisis, you understand firsthand the fragile nature of life.

- You know that pain free days are a gift beyond measure.

- You know the worth of each precious person.

- You know the deep value of shared experiences.

Demonstrate this understanding by appreciating life, by expressing care for the people you encounter, by seeing each event as a never-to-be-repeated opportunity. Enjoy being and growing with your child. Cherish time with family members and friends who are dear to you. Be a genuine and caring friend.

Refuse to call your crisis good. Instead notice and cherish God's provision of joy in the midst of crisis. Then live in ways that bring God's good to the here and now. Choose hope instead of despair, freedom instead of restriction, life instead of death.

211

Choosing joy is more than a faith move. It makes every area of life better. Doctors have repeatedly documented the healing capacity of laughter and positive thoughts. An atmosphere of joy and willingness to see the good can not only empower your child but also heal your family, your past, and your present.

There really is hope. We really can choose joy.

"This day I call heaven and earth as witnesses against you that I have set before you life and death, blessings and curses. Now choose life, so that you and your children may live and that you may love the Lord your God, listen to his voice, and hold fast to him. For the Lord is your life, and he will give you many years in the land he swore to give your fathers, Abraham, Isaac and Jacob" (Deut. 30:19-20).

THE POINT ⟵

Diseases, disabilities, accidents, and death are a few of the many ways Satan tries to steal our joy. His efforts do bring deep pain. But God is stronger. Because of God we can experience God's abundant life in the middle of this very imperfect world.

"The thief comes only to steal and kill and destroy; I have come that they may have life, and have it to the full." (John 10:10)